URBAN WORLD
Volume I

PHOTOS BY

DAVID GALLIE

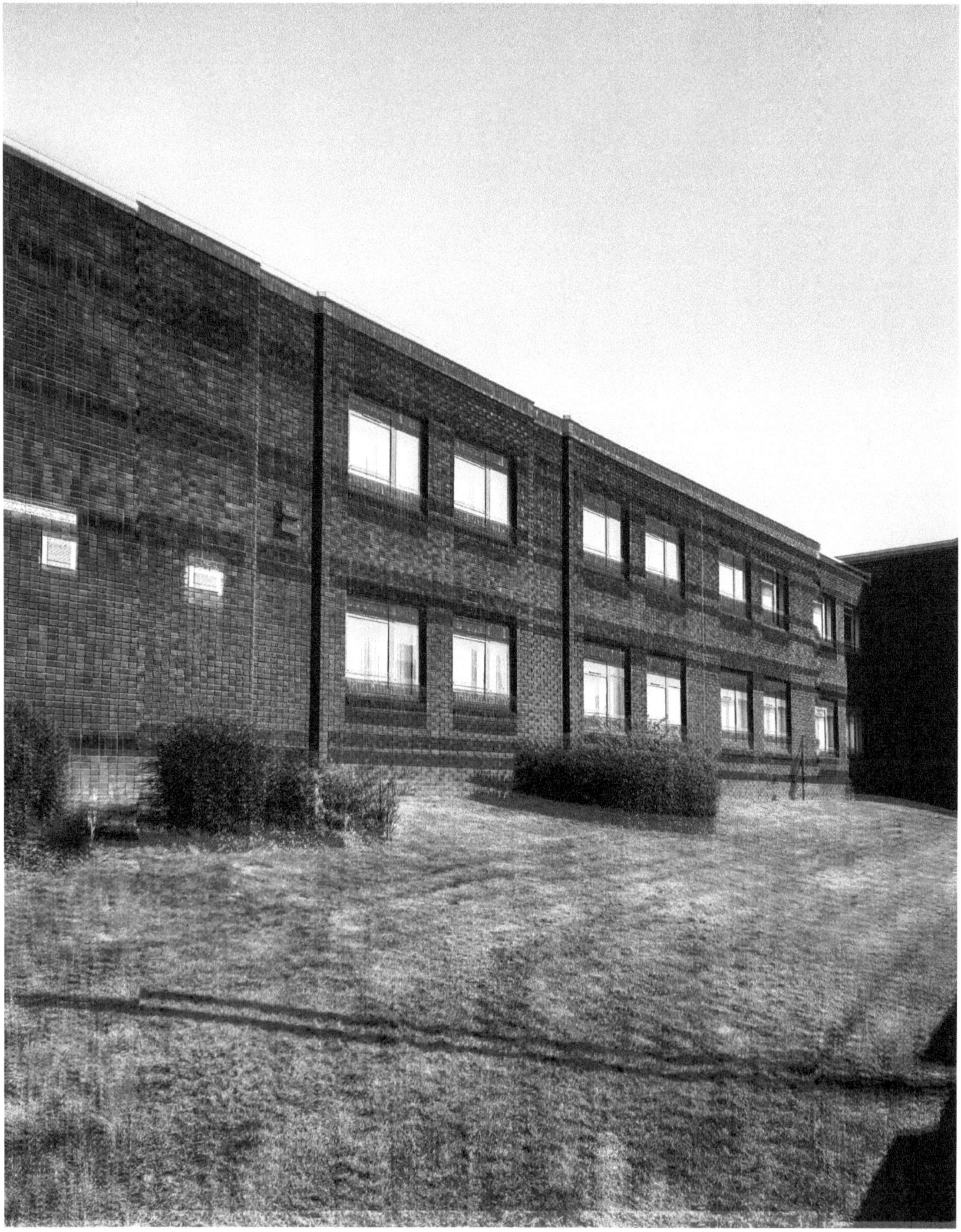

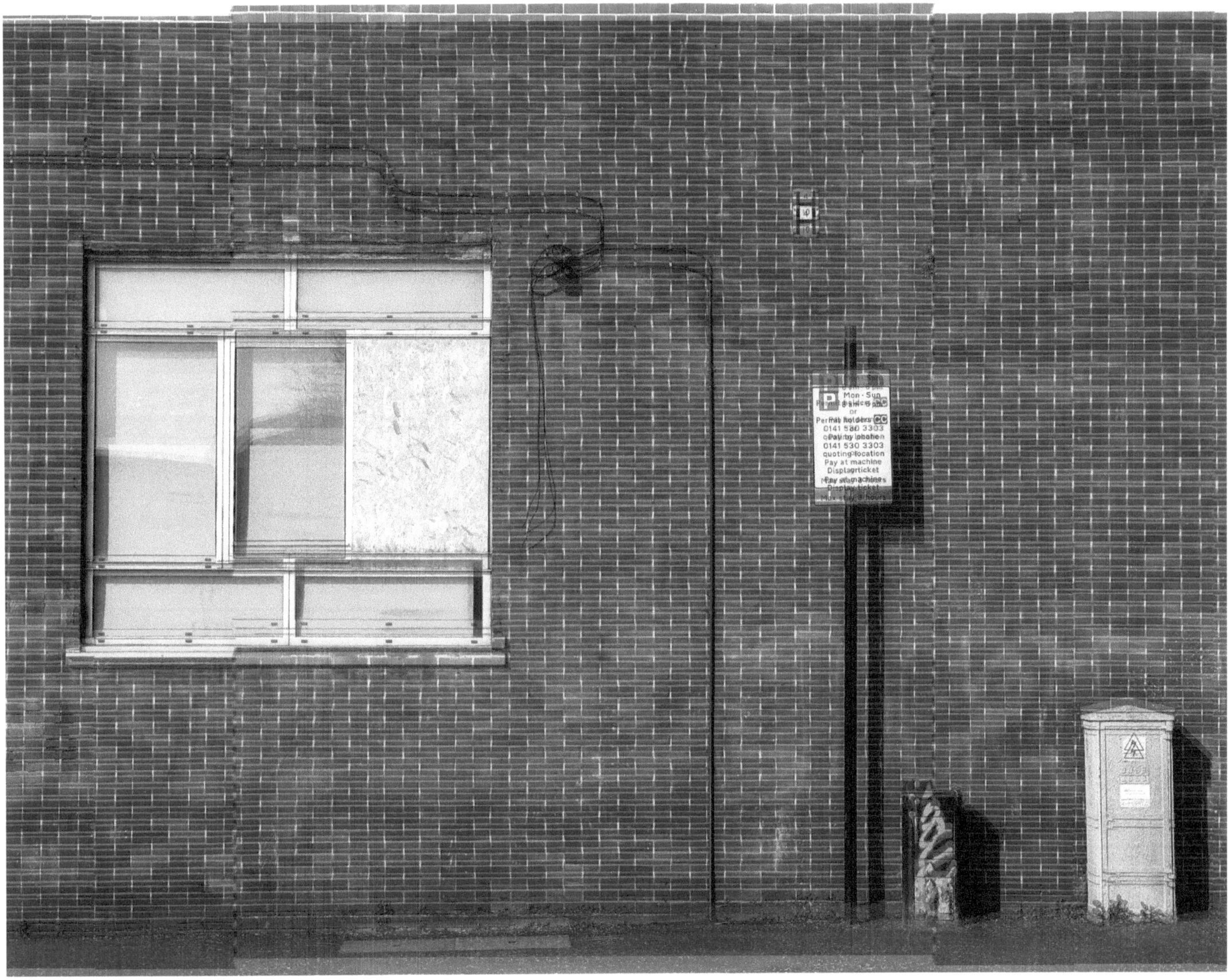
P
Mon - Sun
or
CC
0141 530 3303
quoting location
Pay at machine

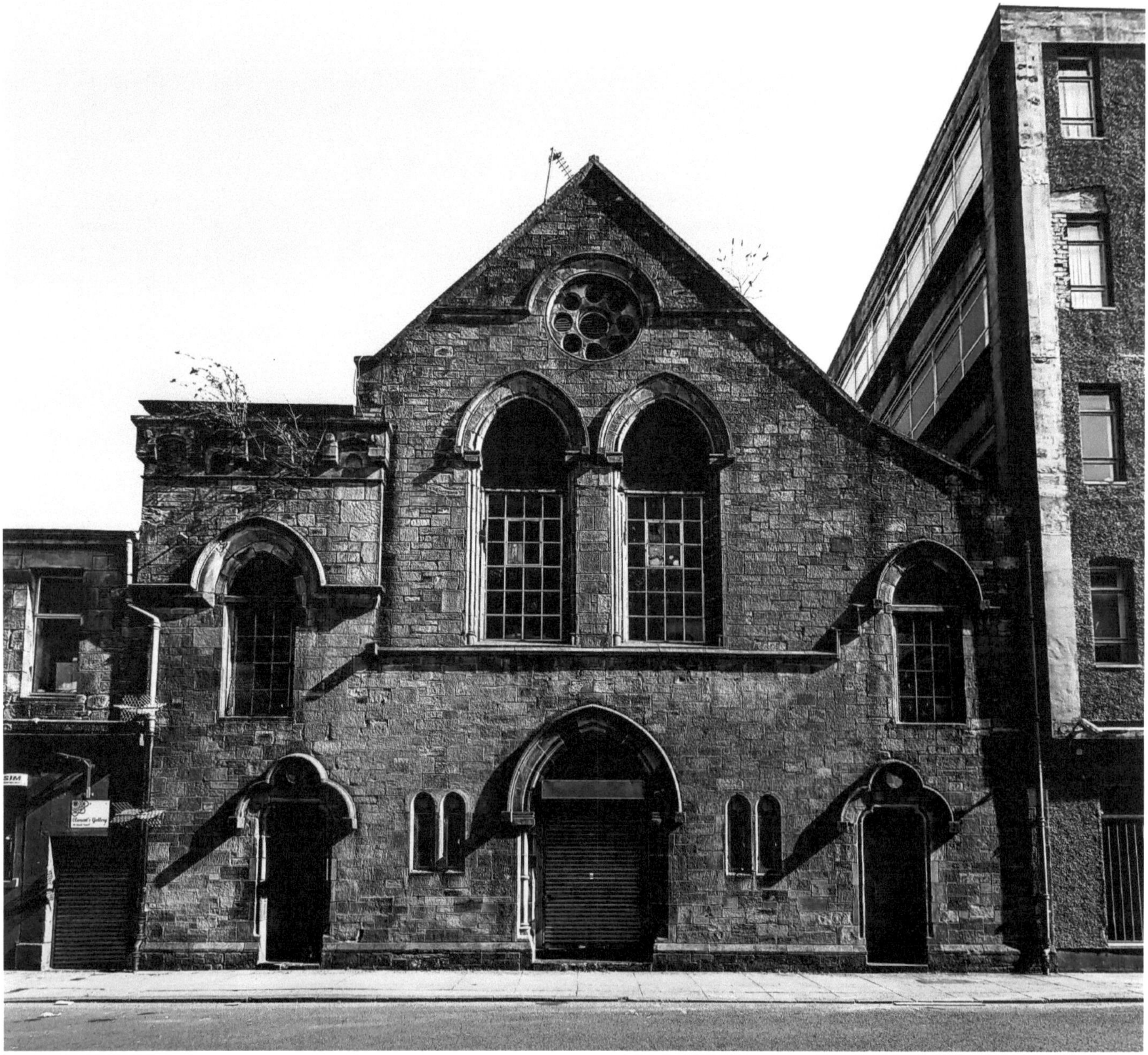
SIM

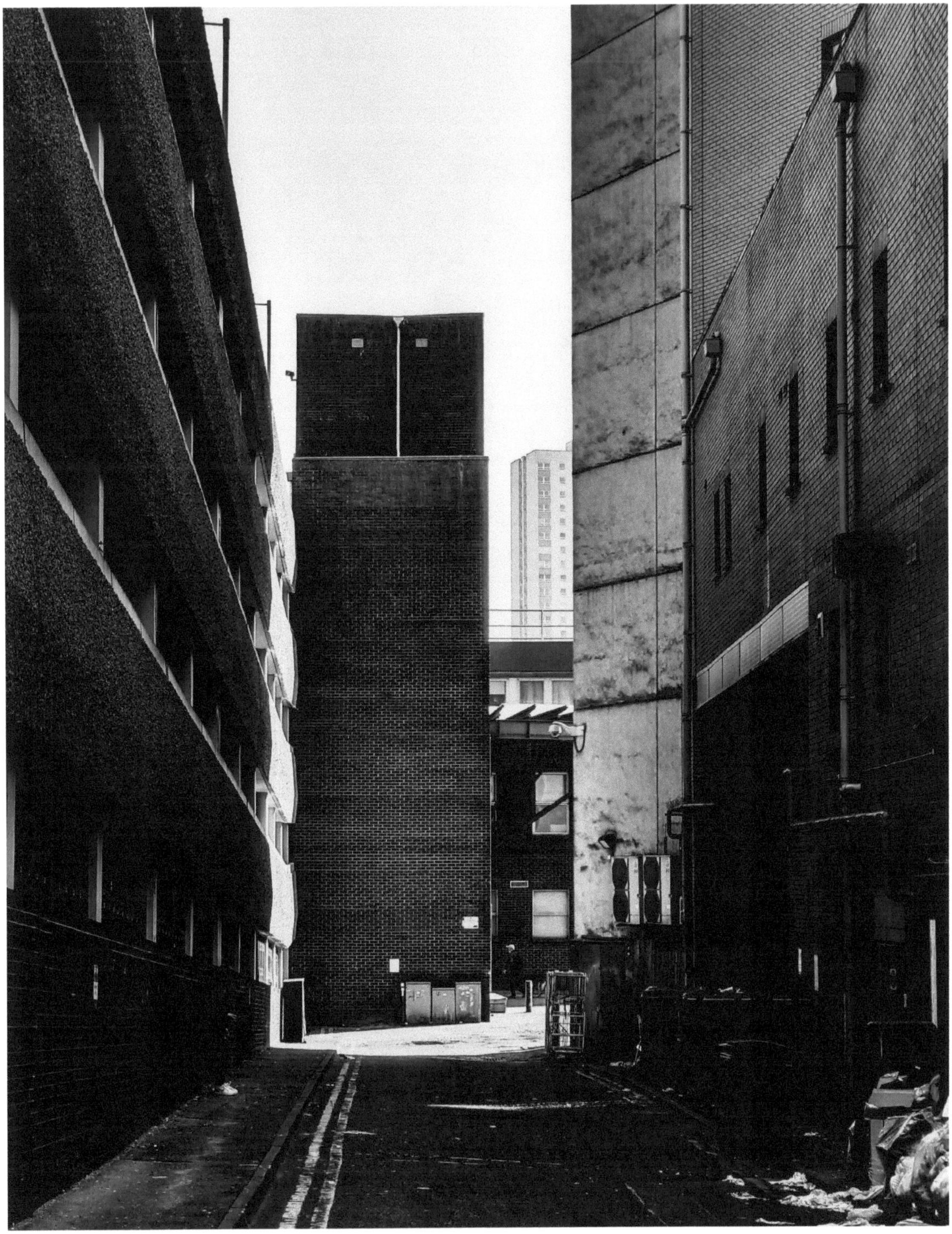

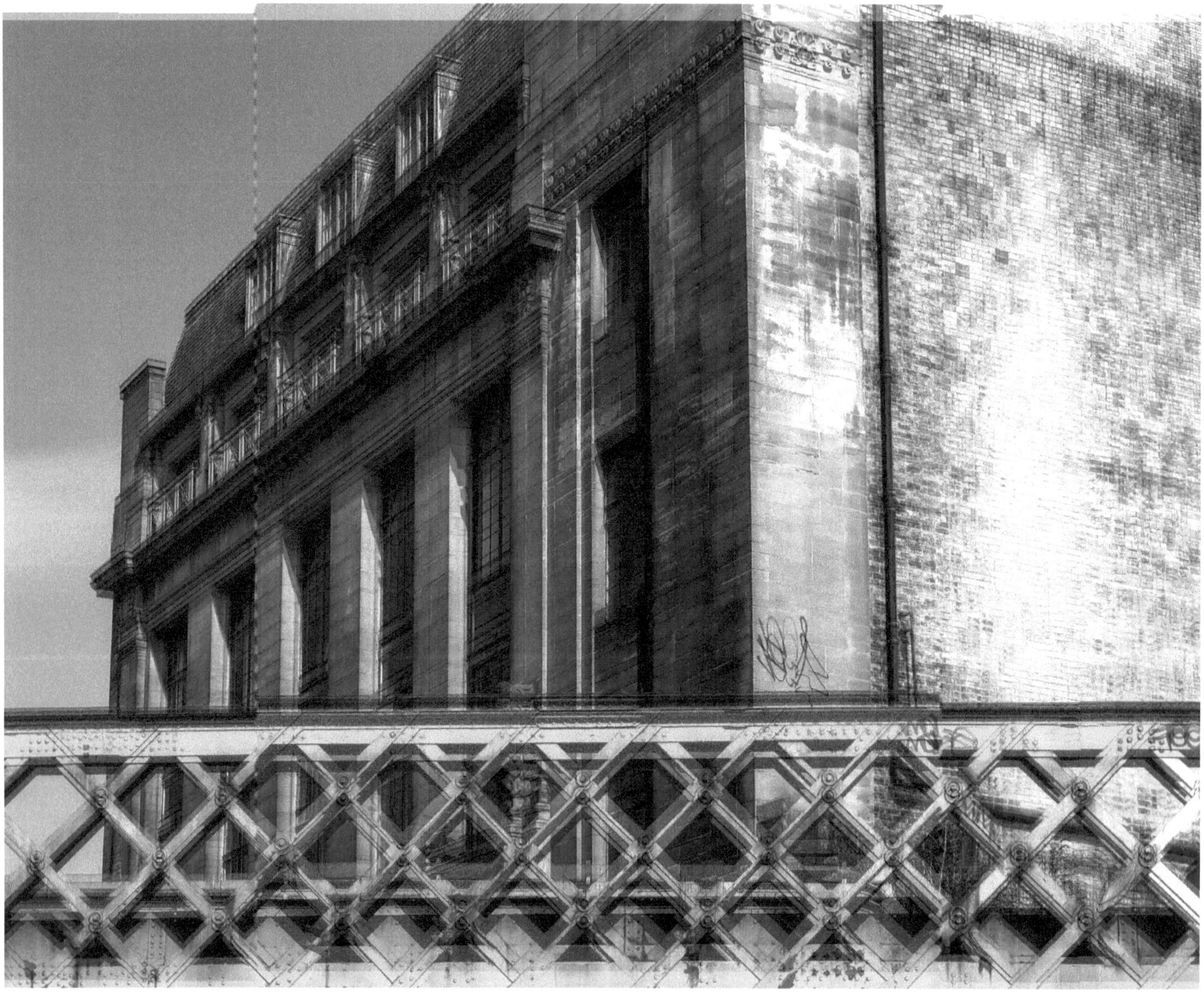

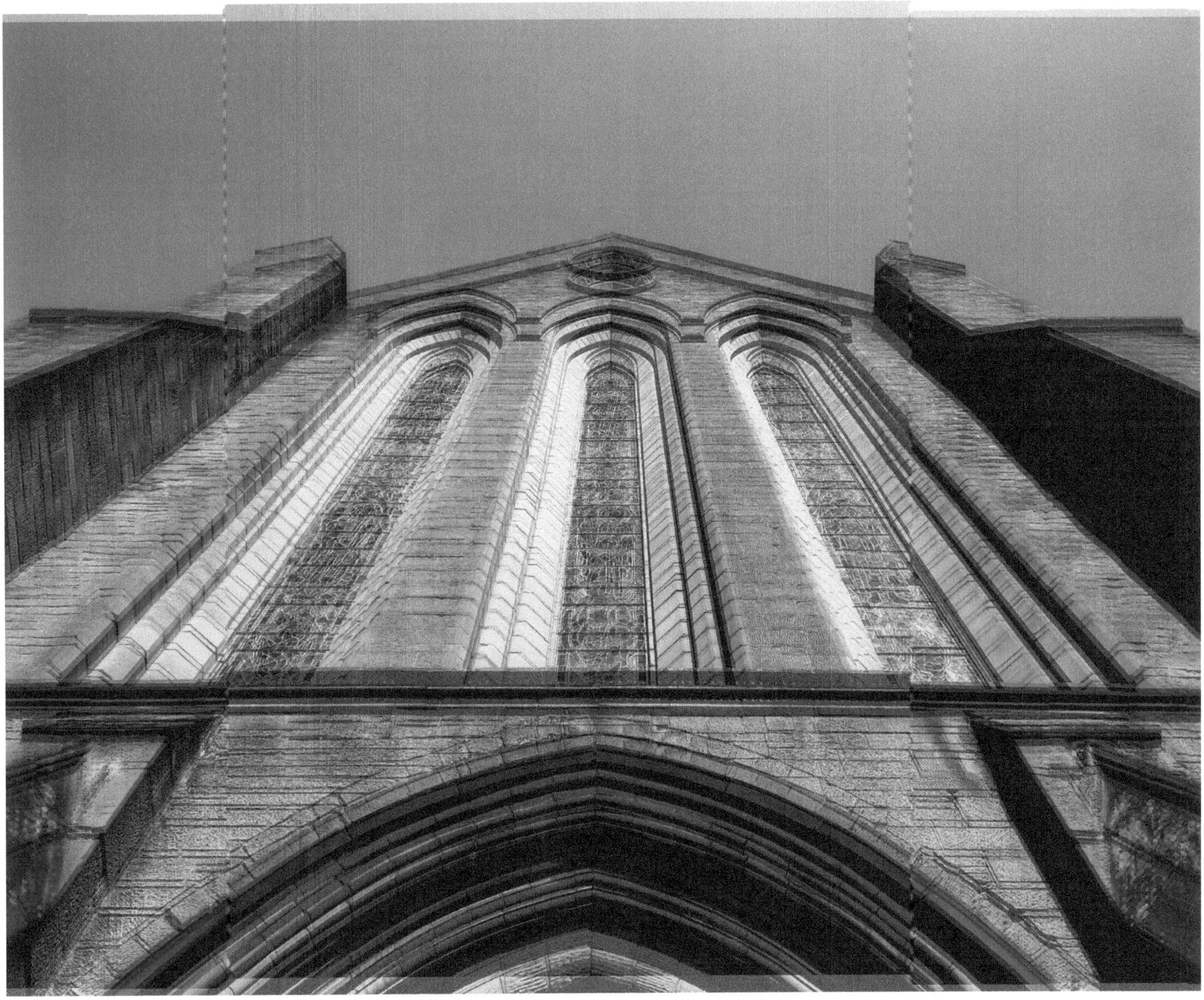

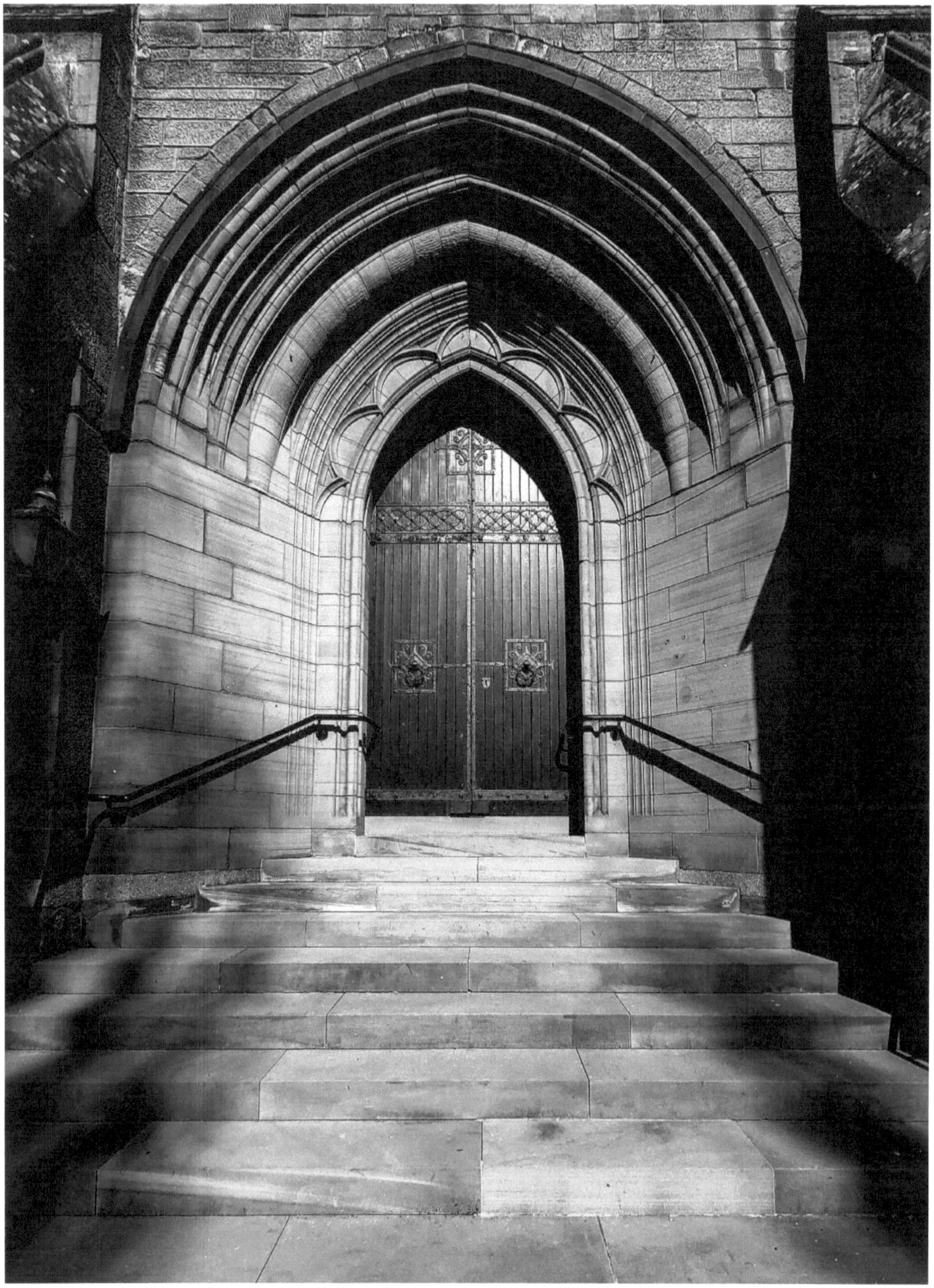

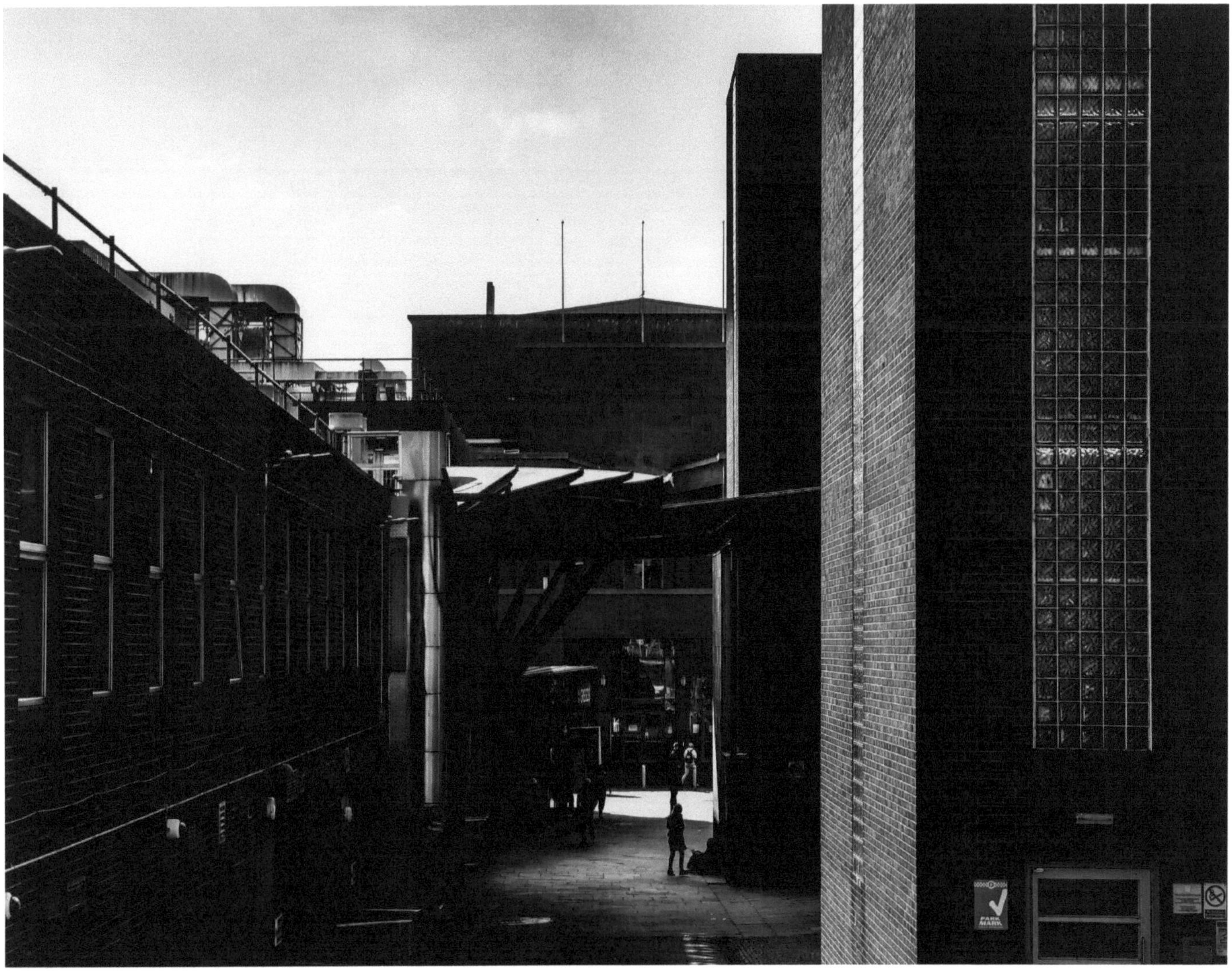
PARK MARK

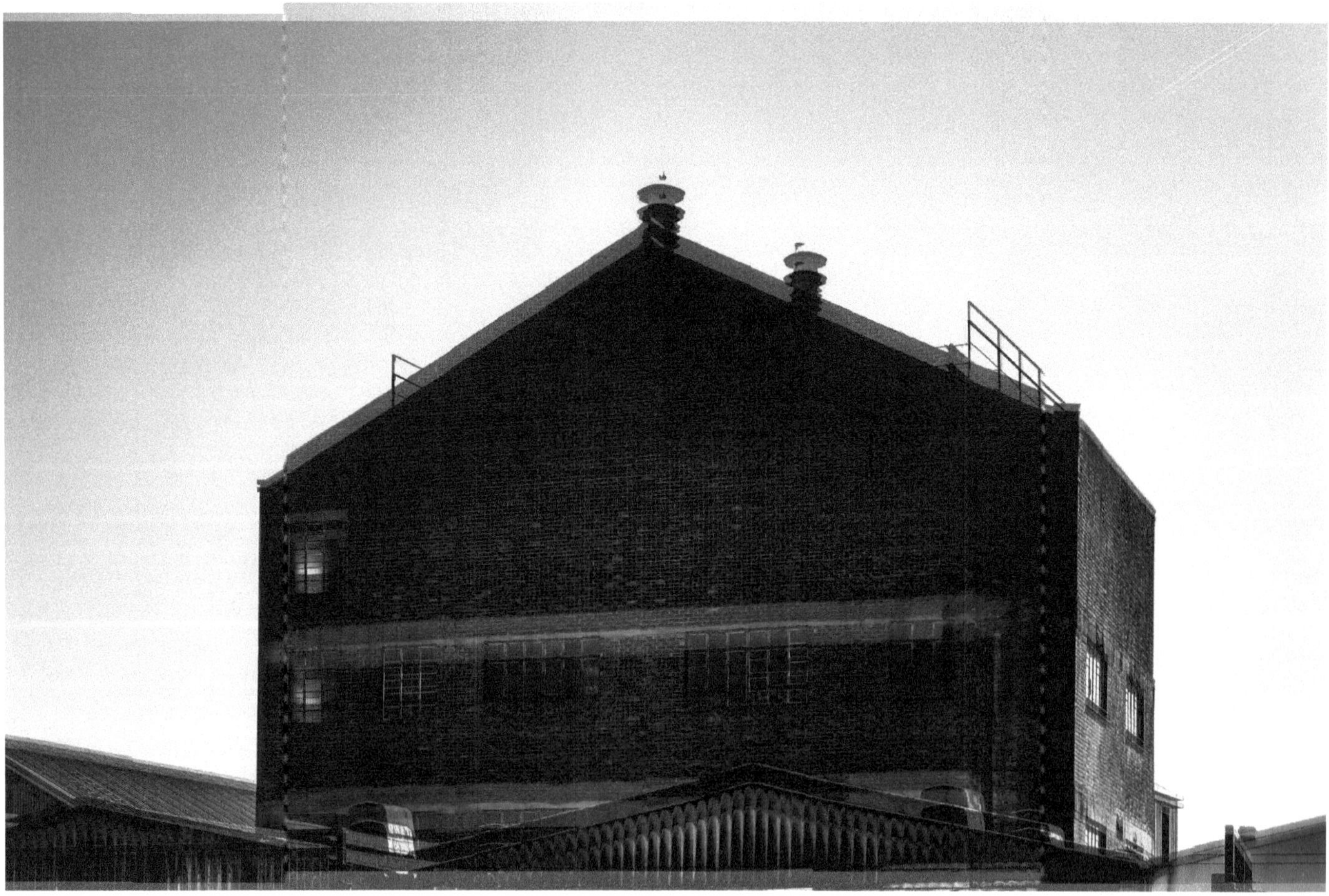

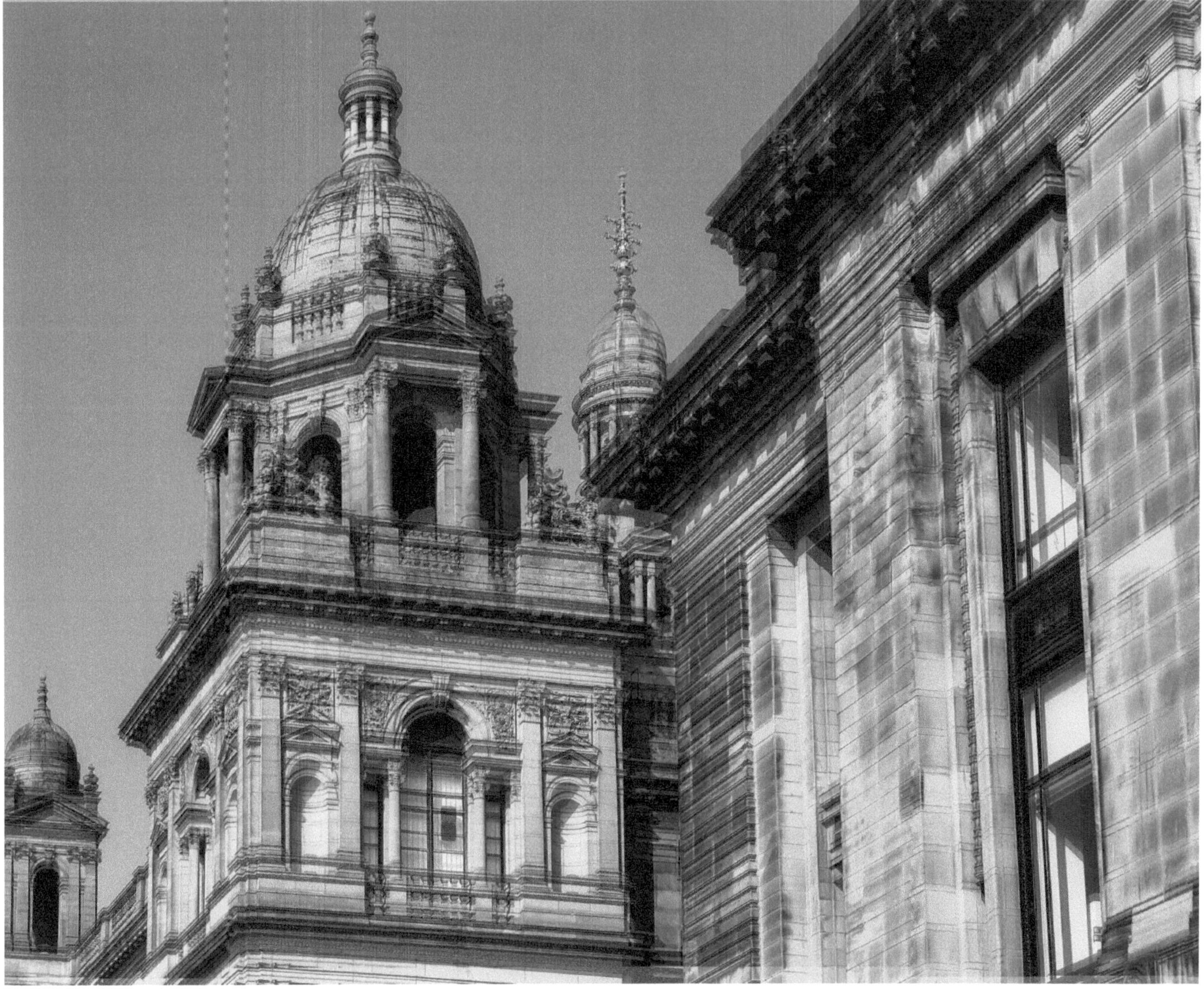

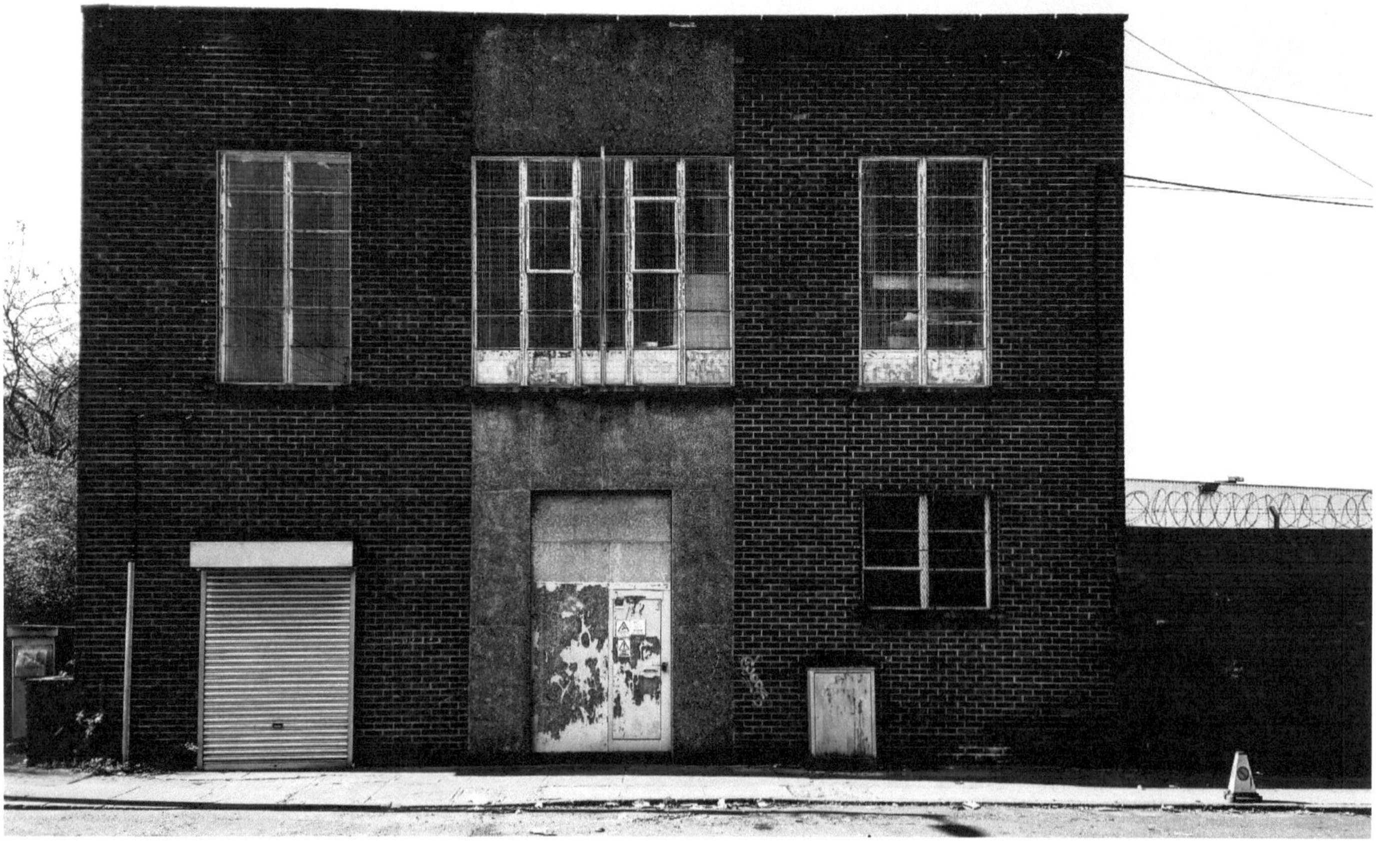

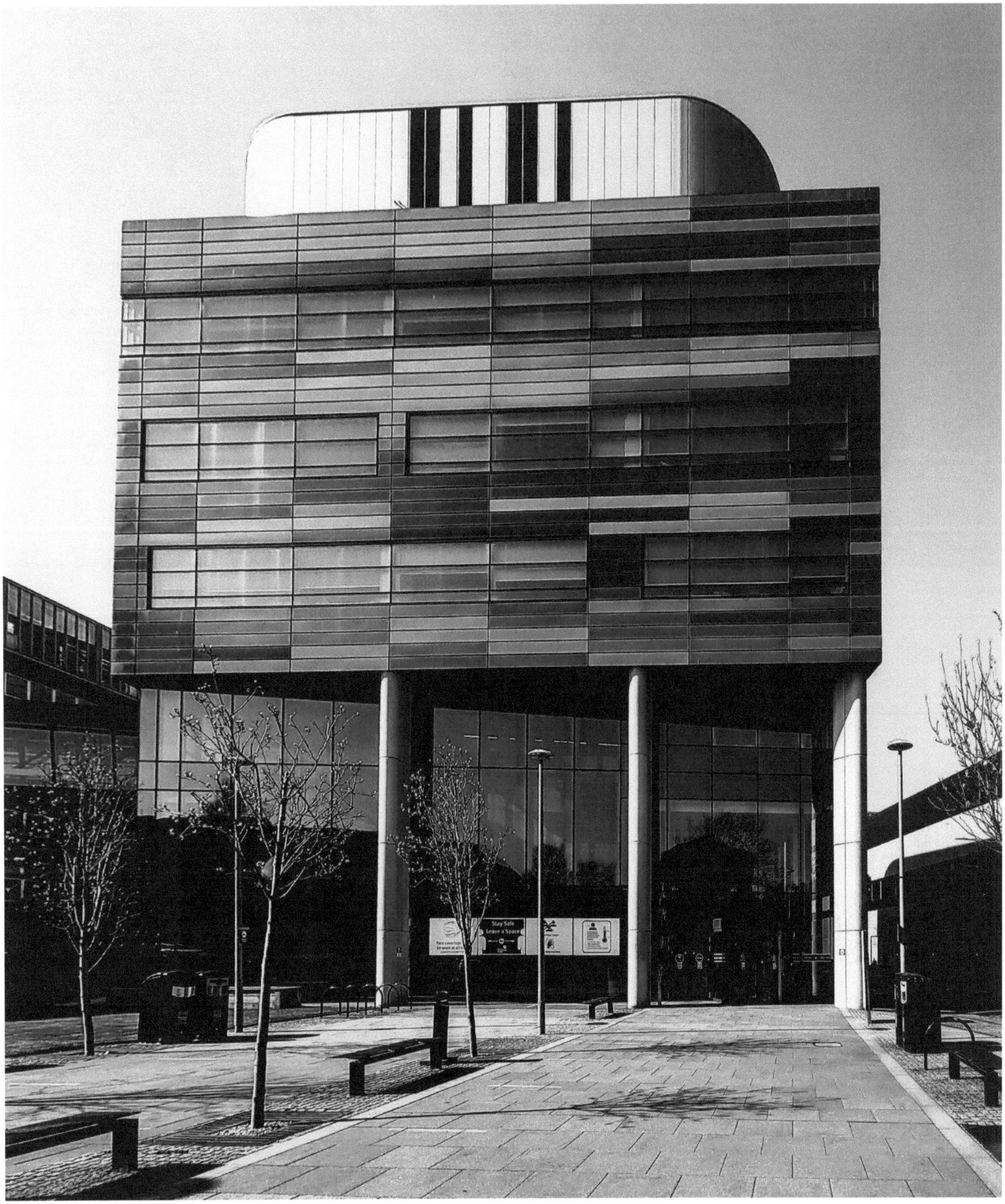
Stay Safe
Leave a Space

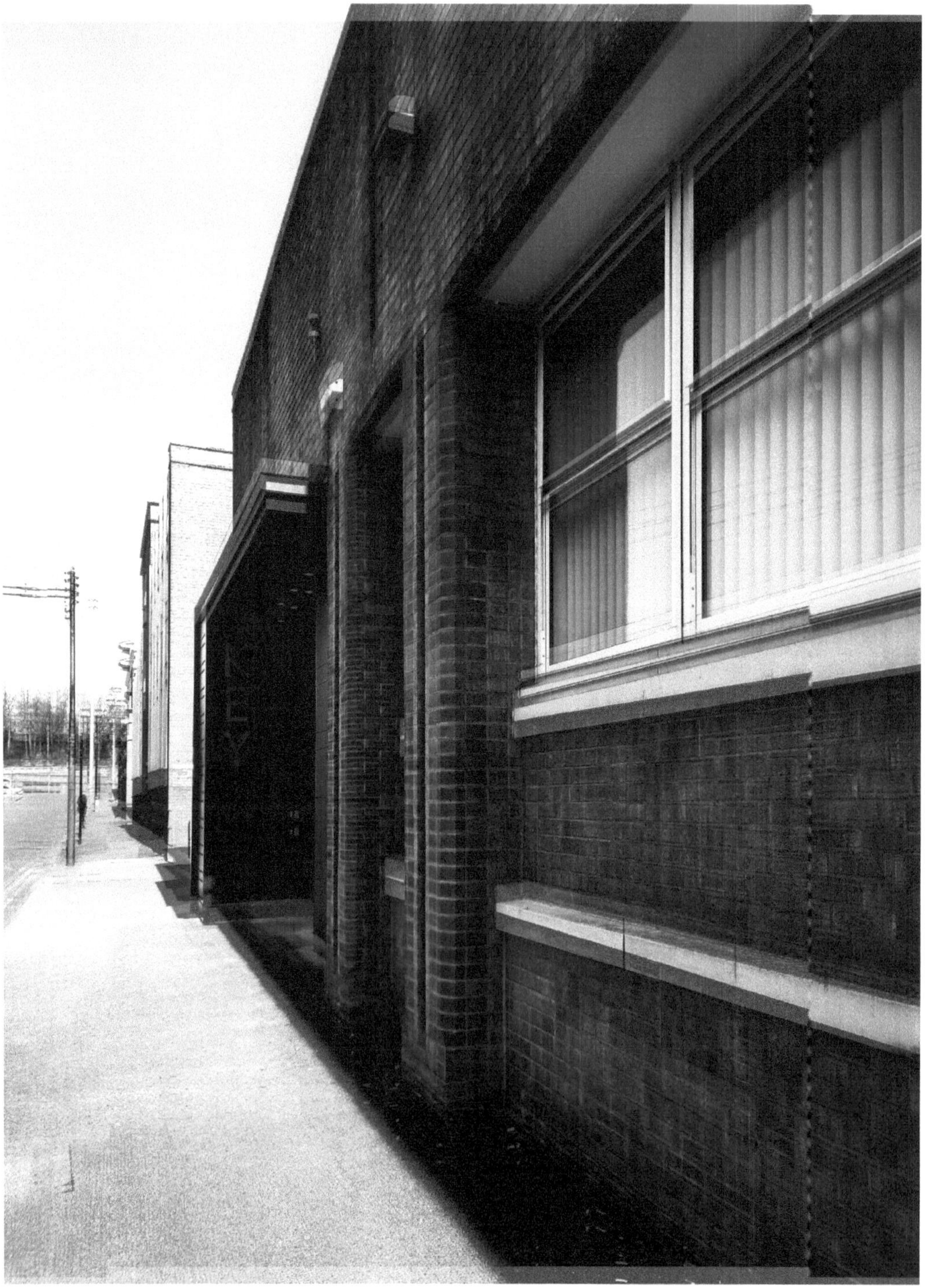

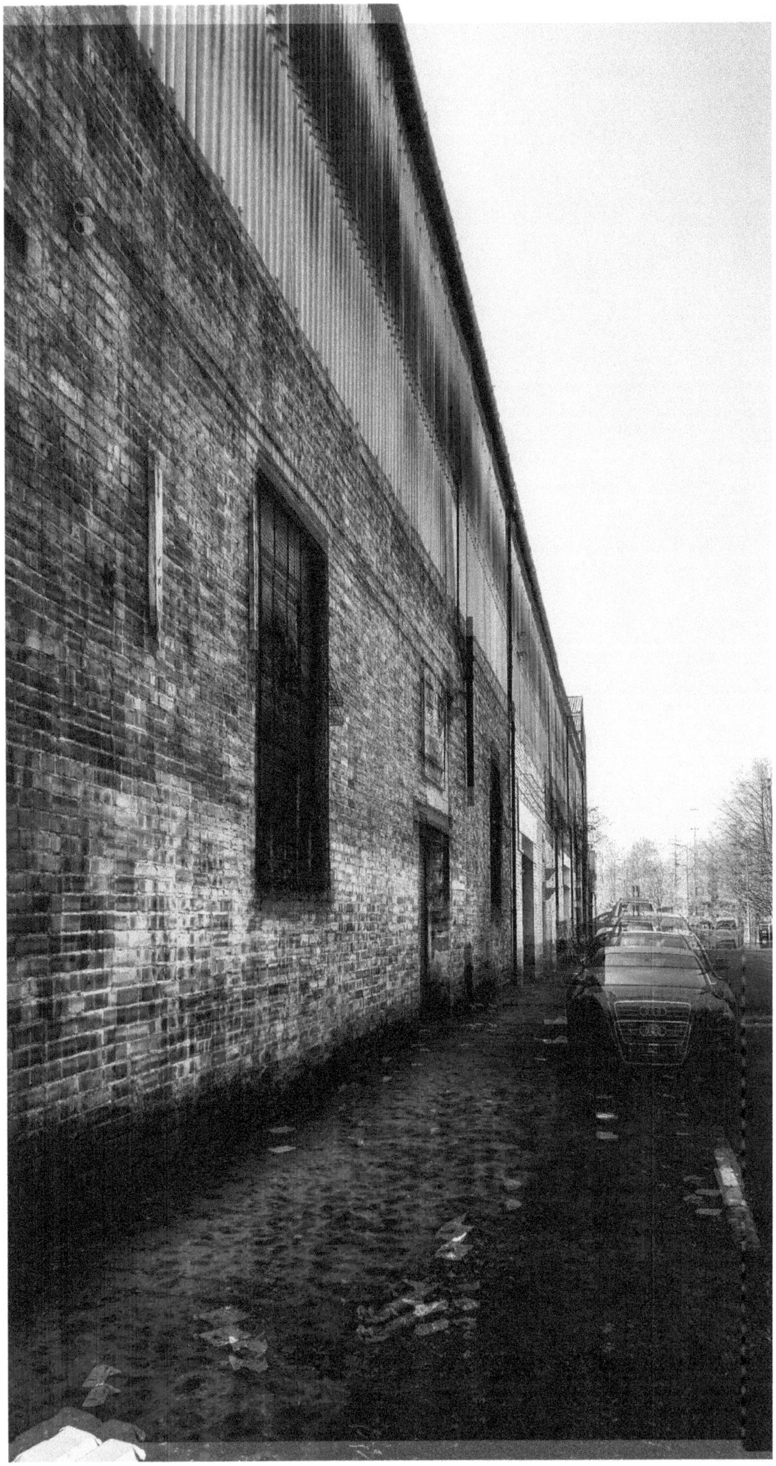

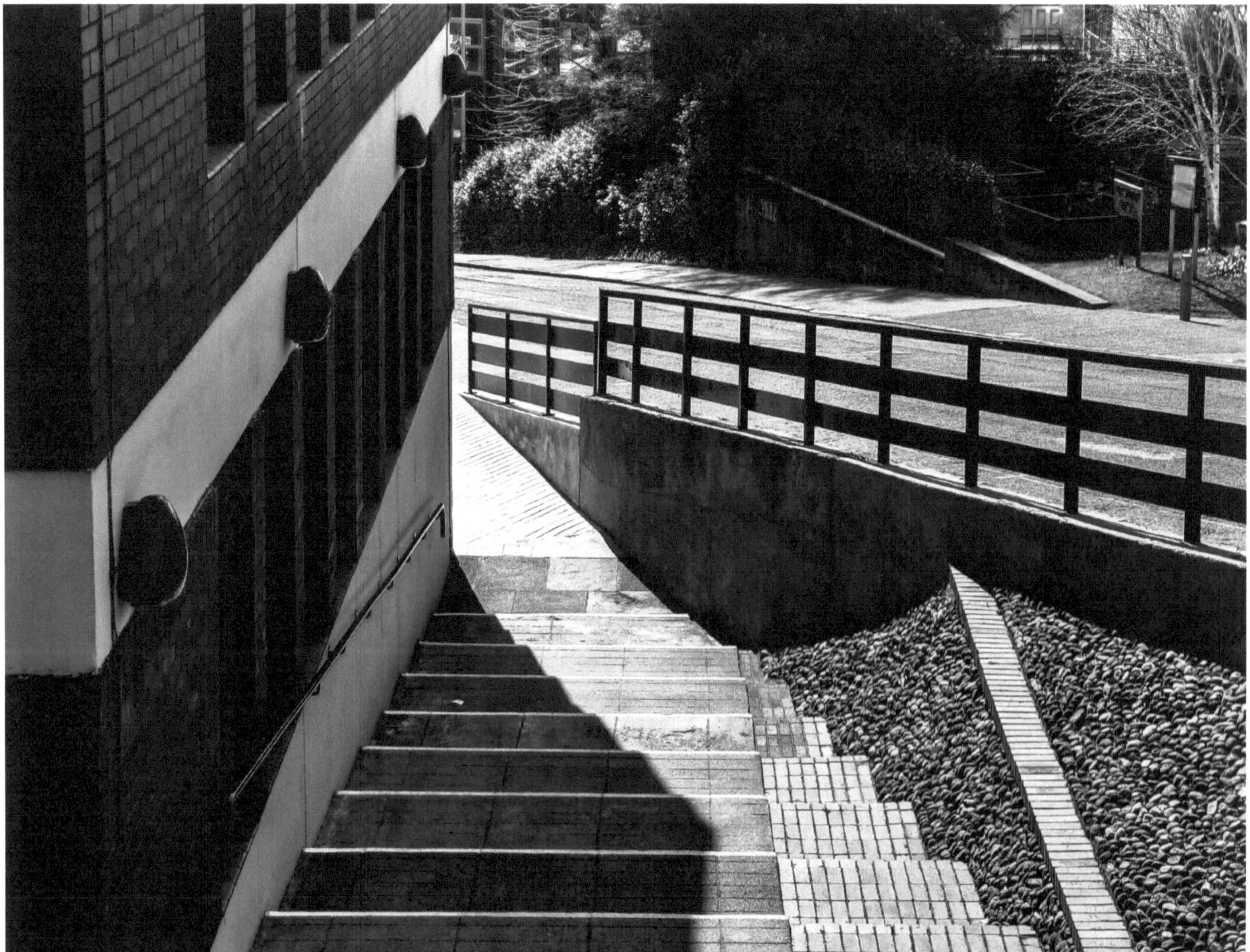

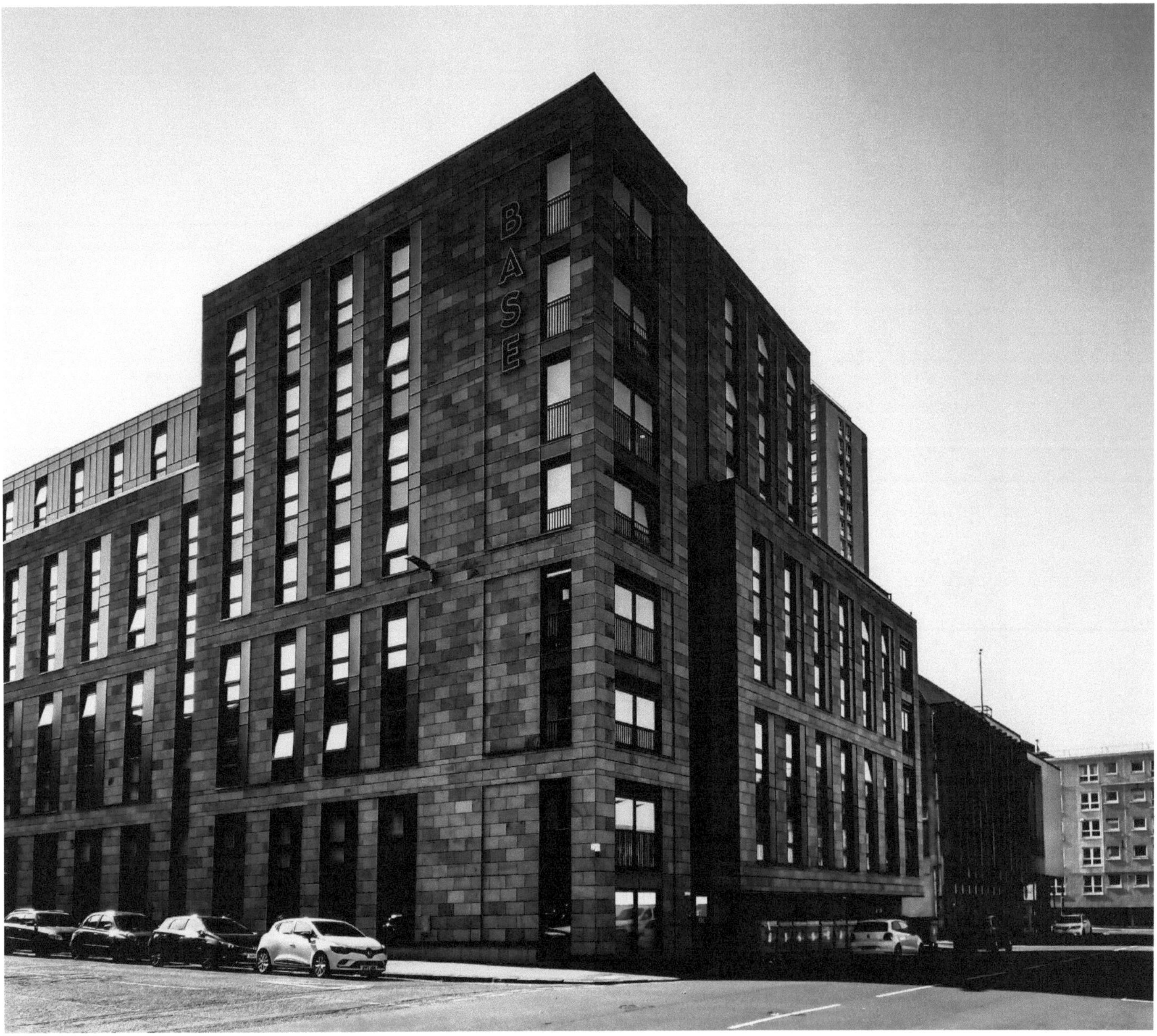
BASE

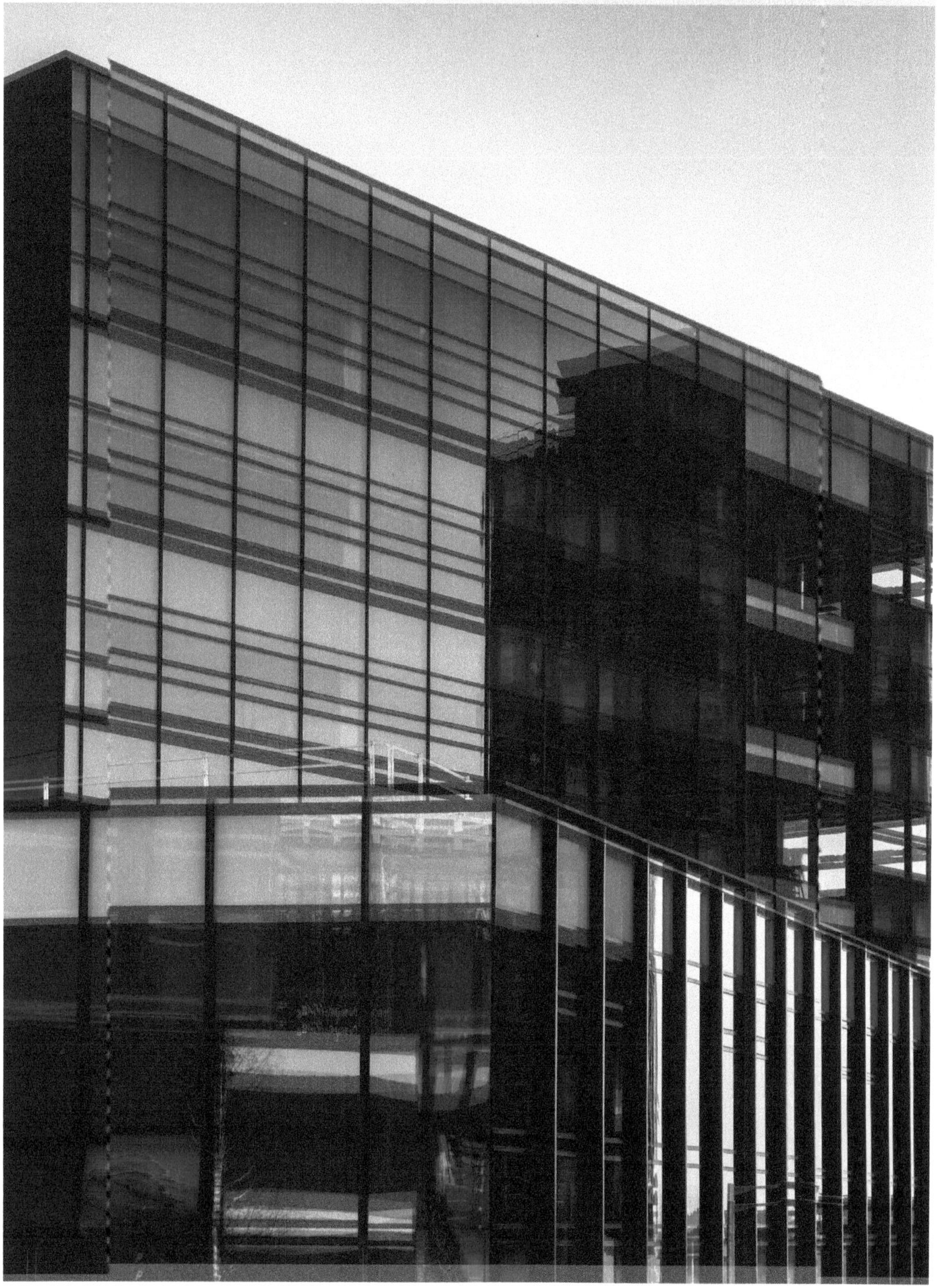

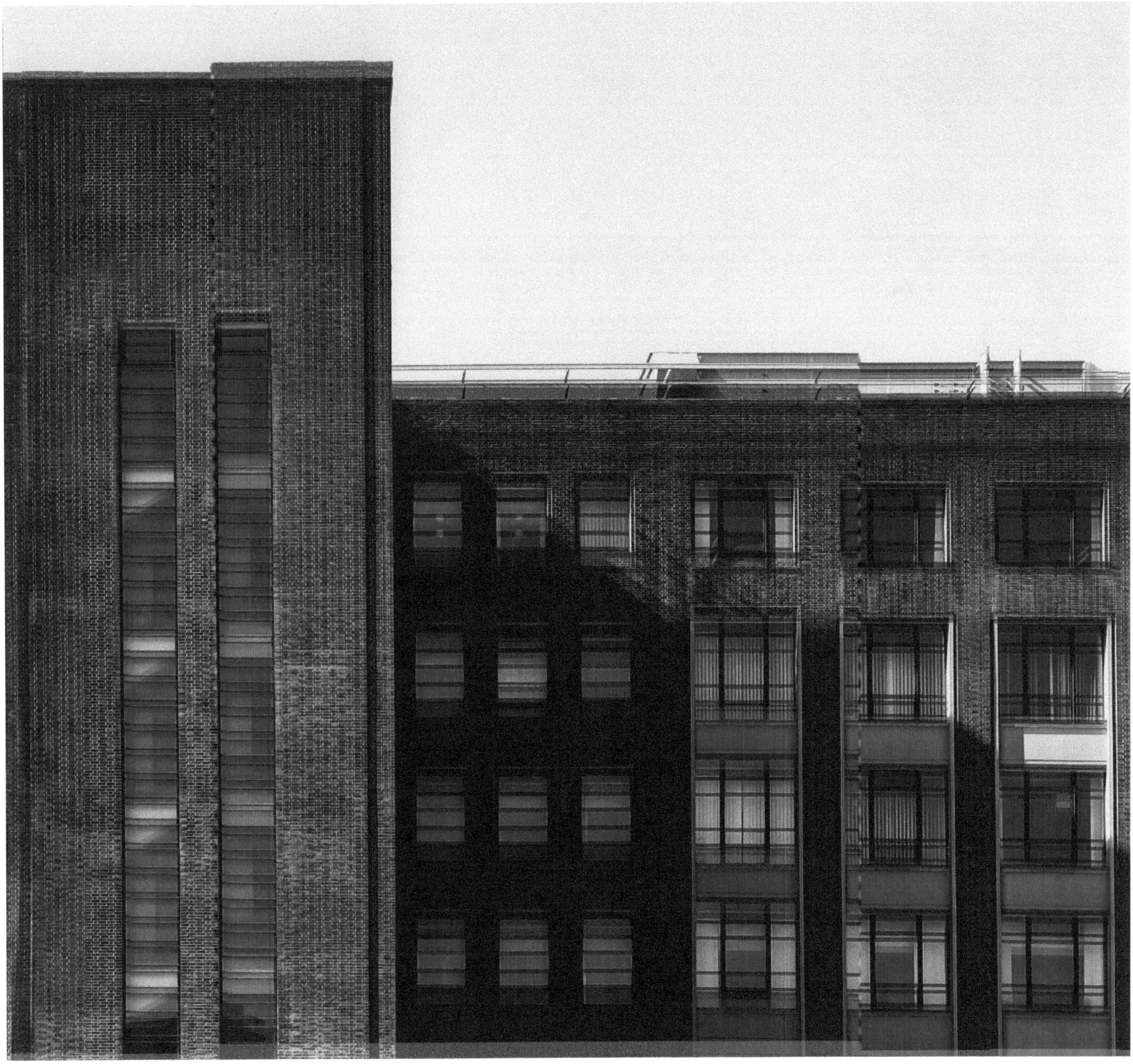

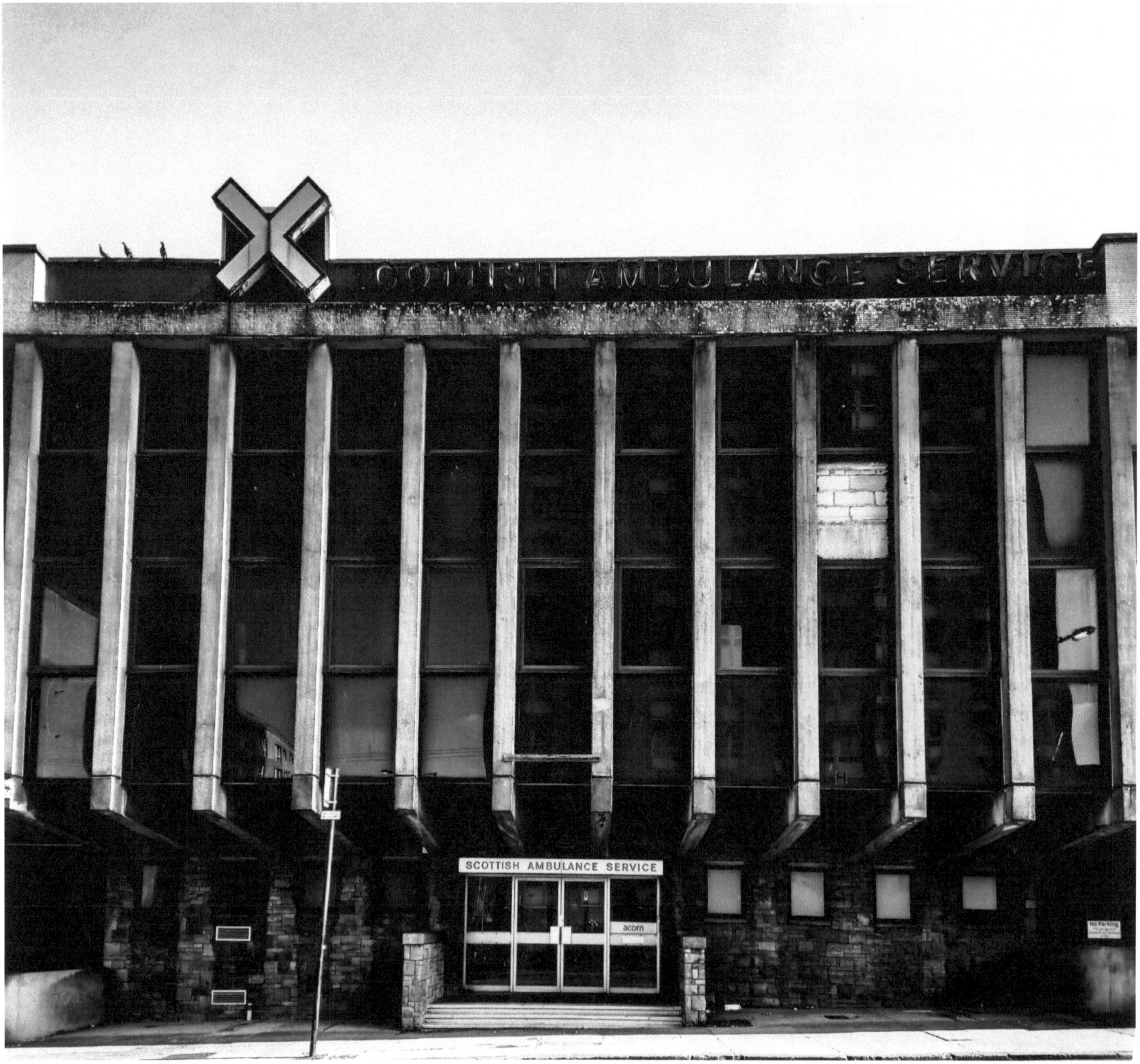
SCOTTISH AMBULANCE SERVICE
acorn
No Parking

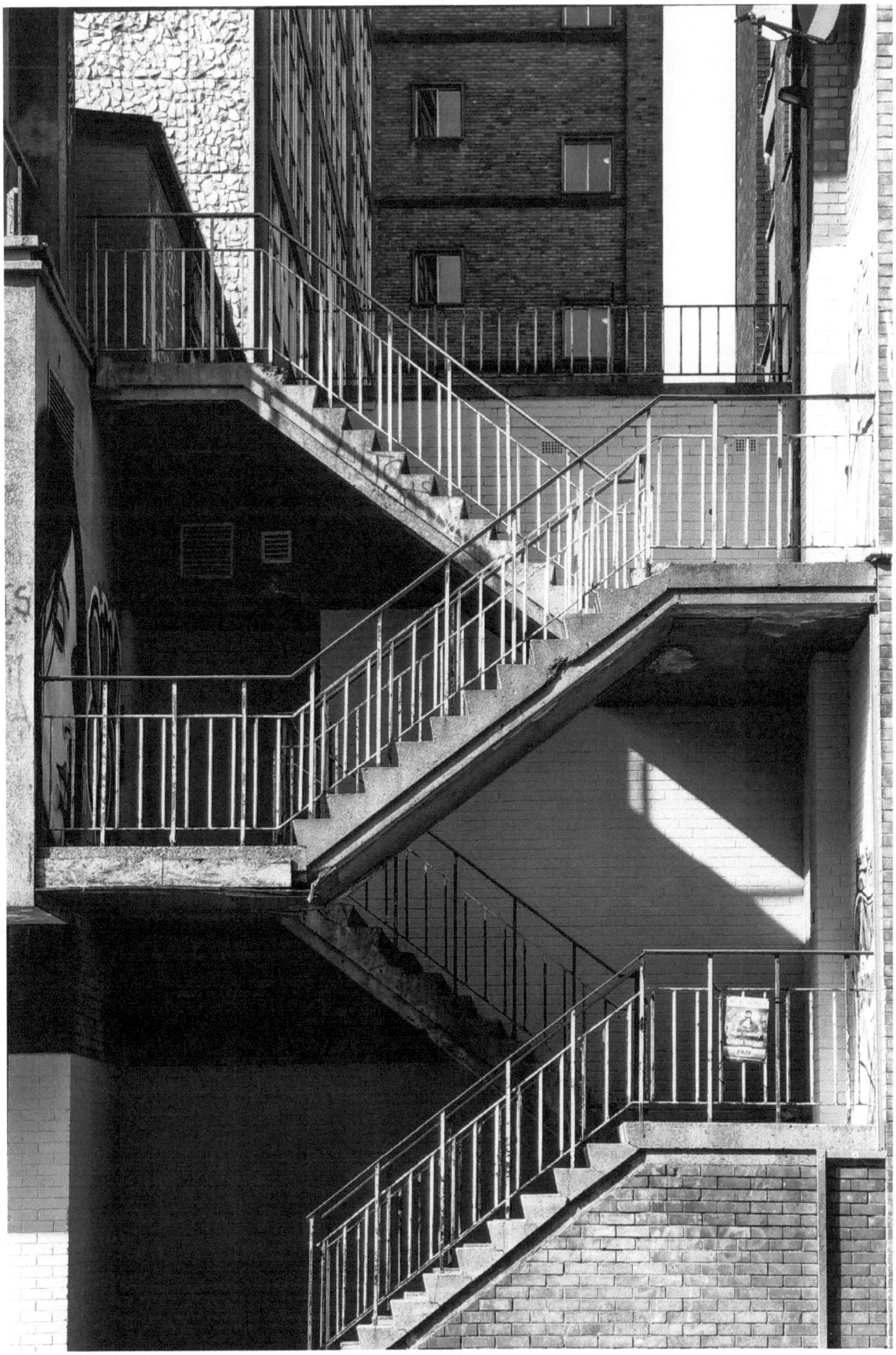

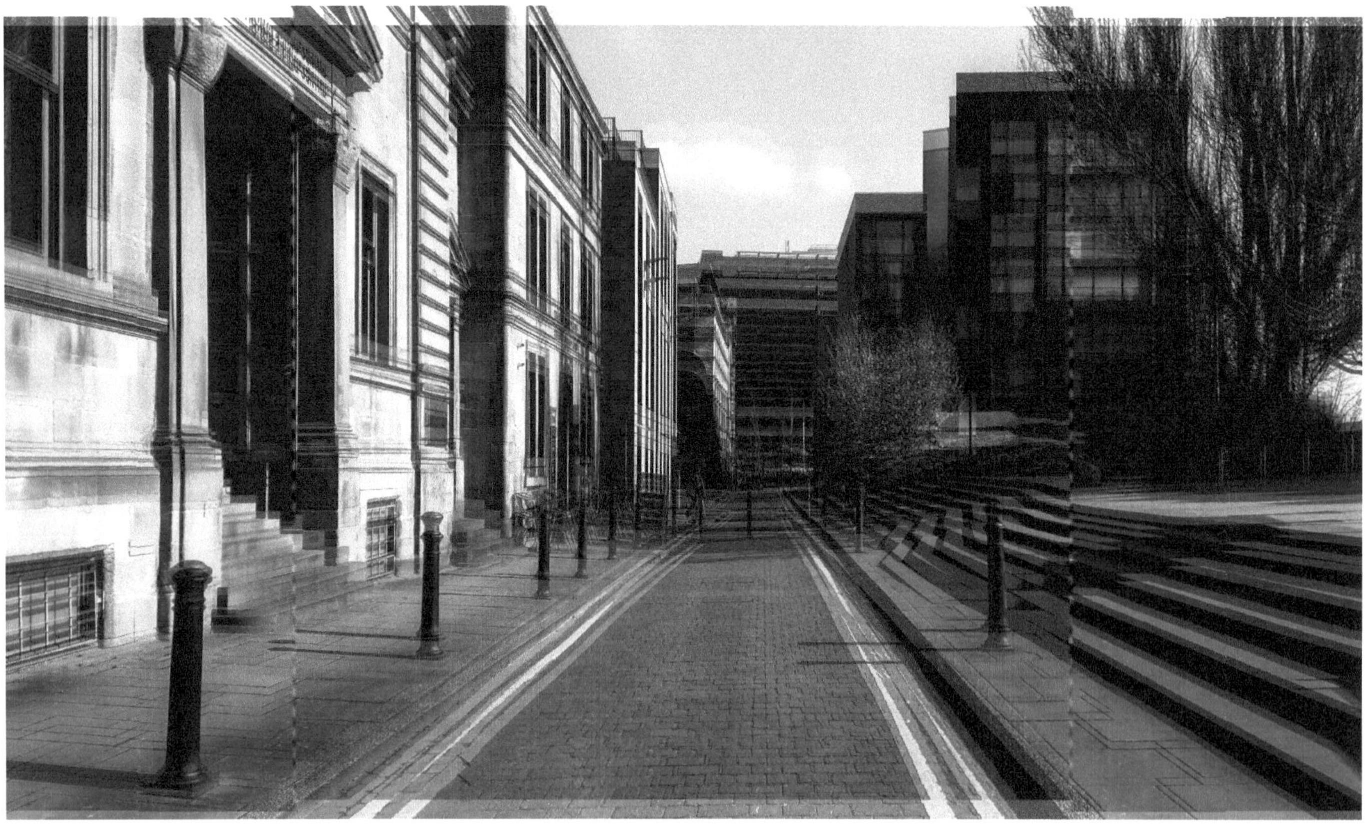

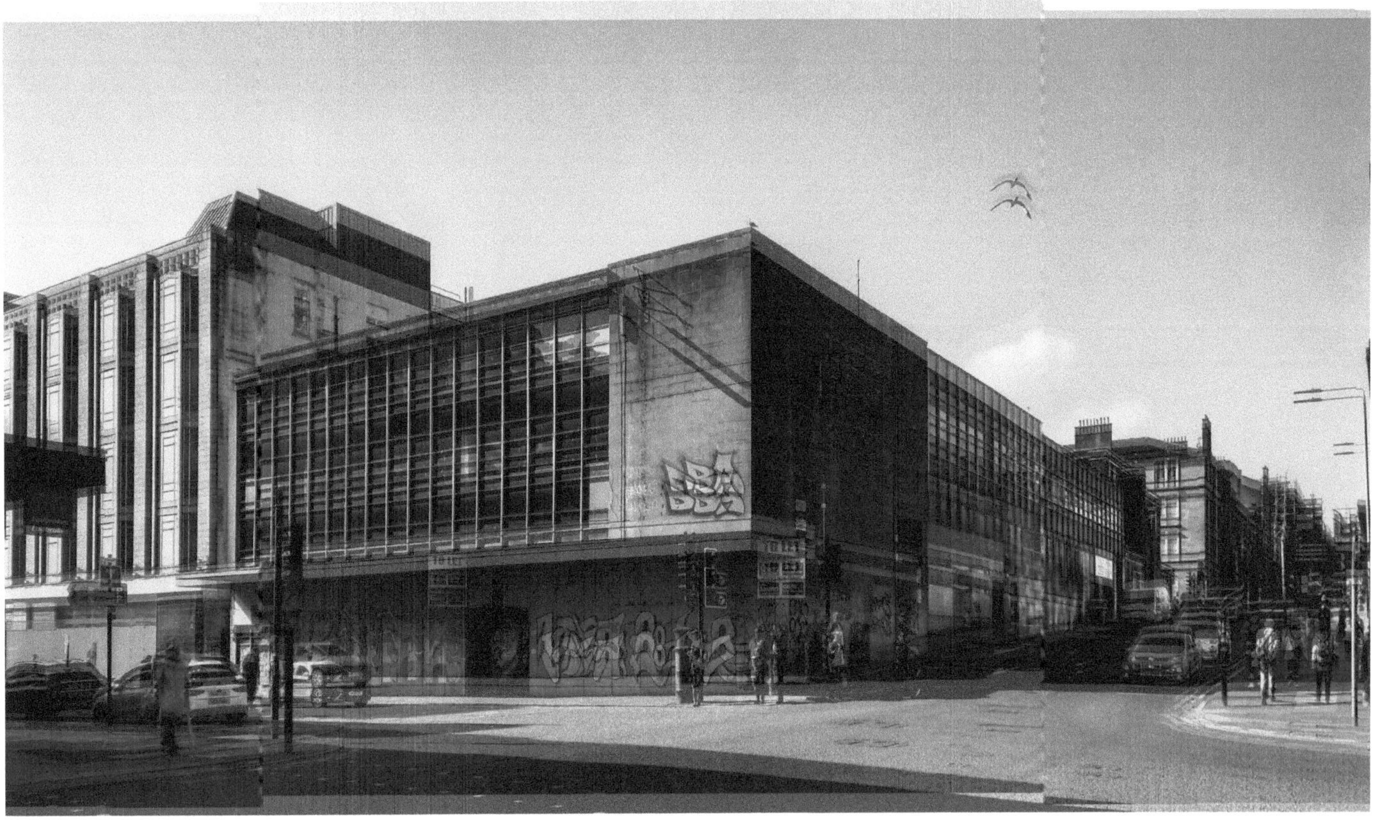

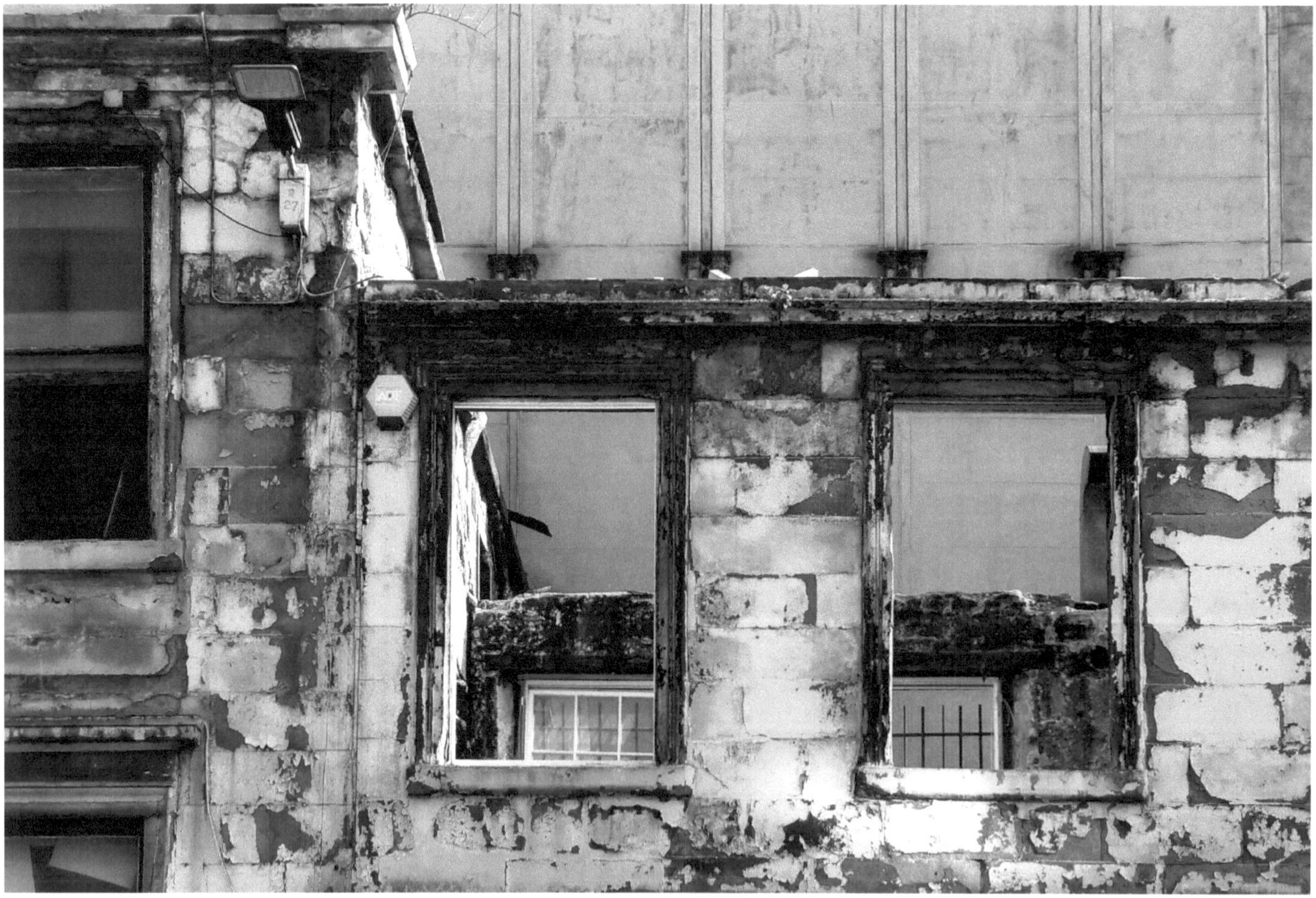

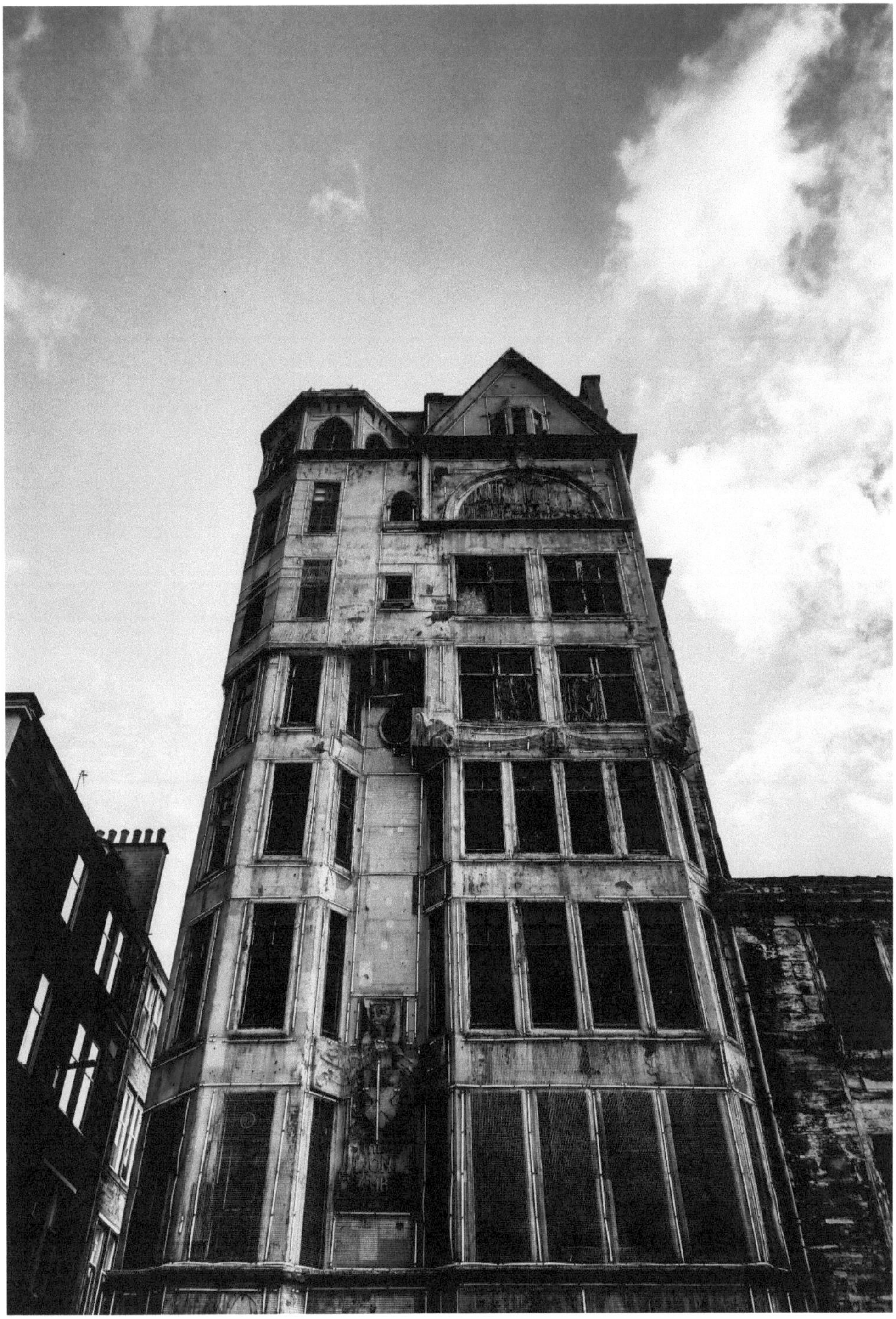

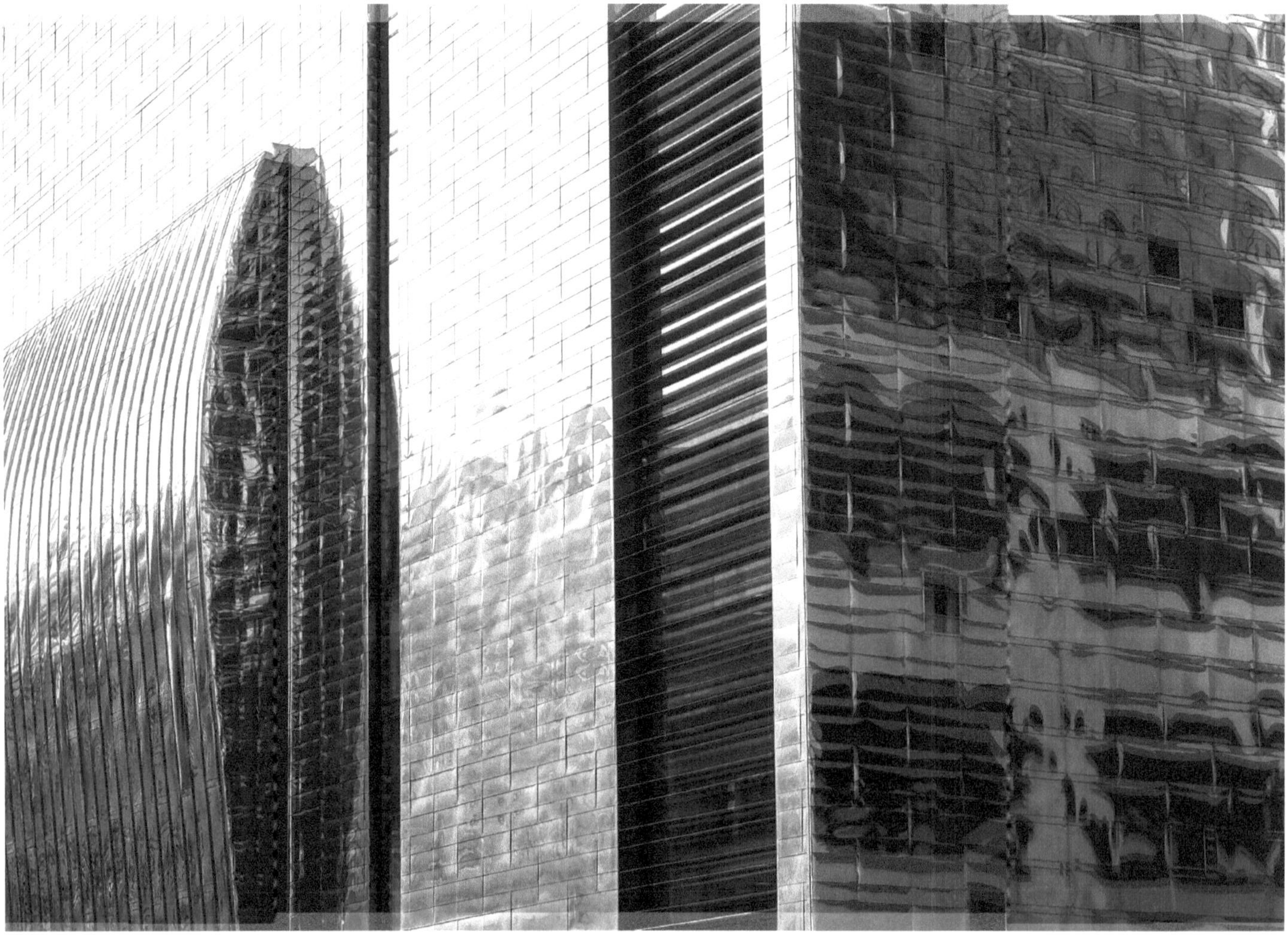

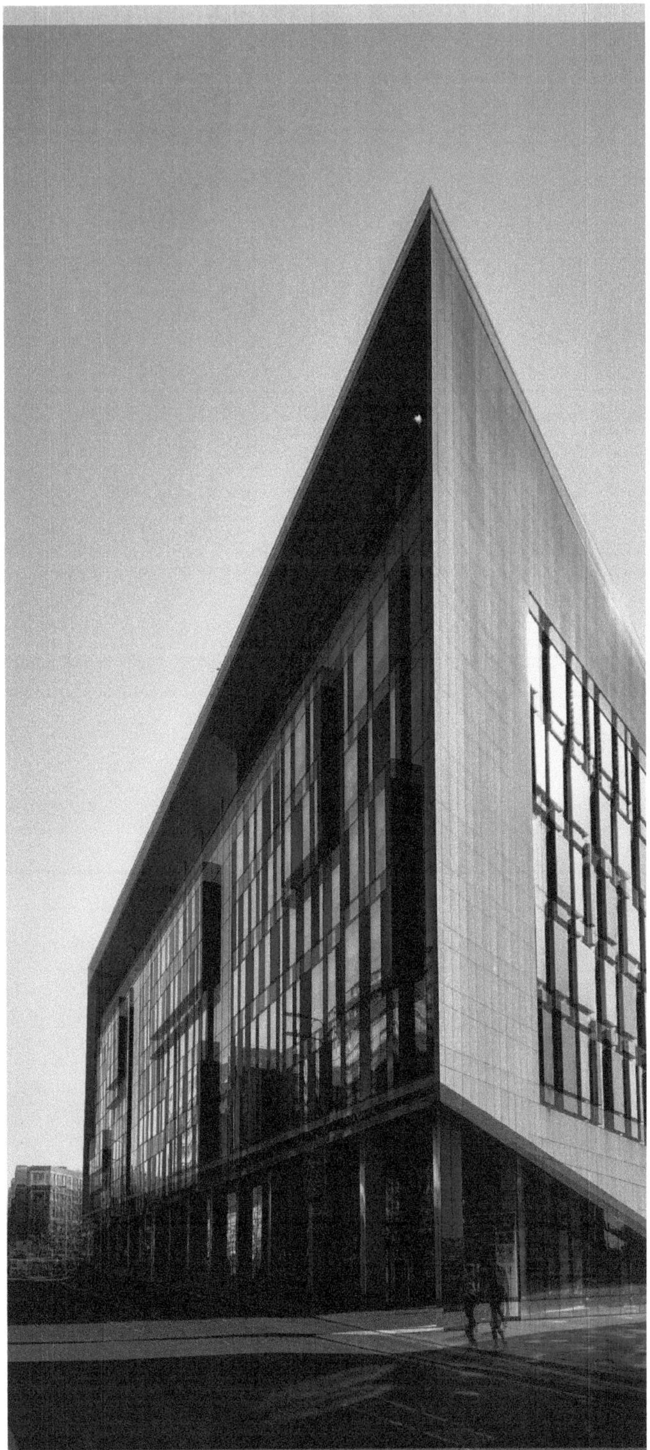

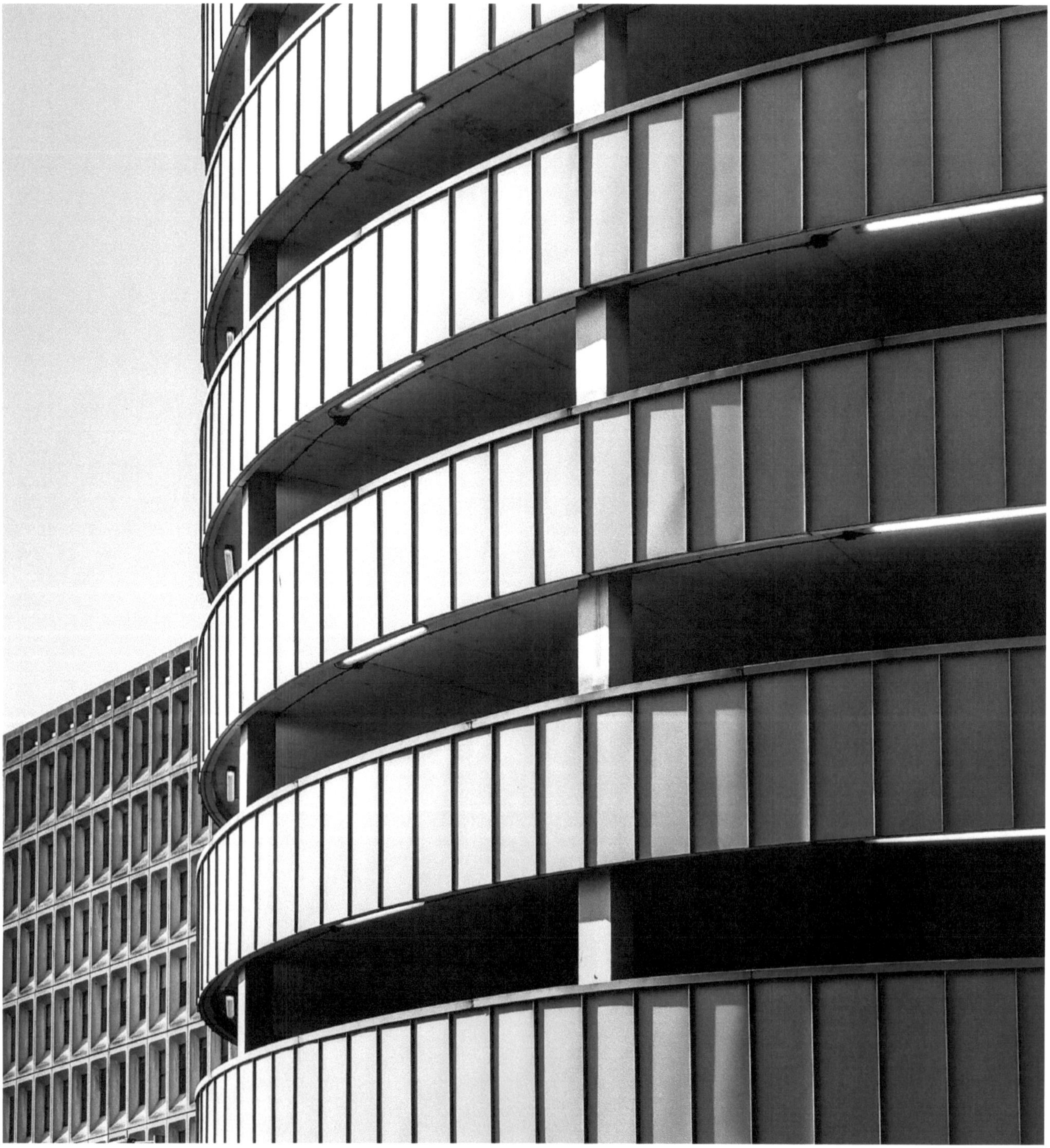

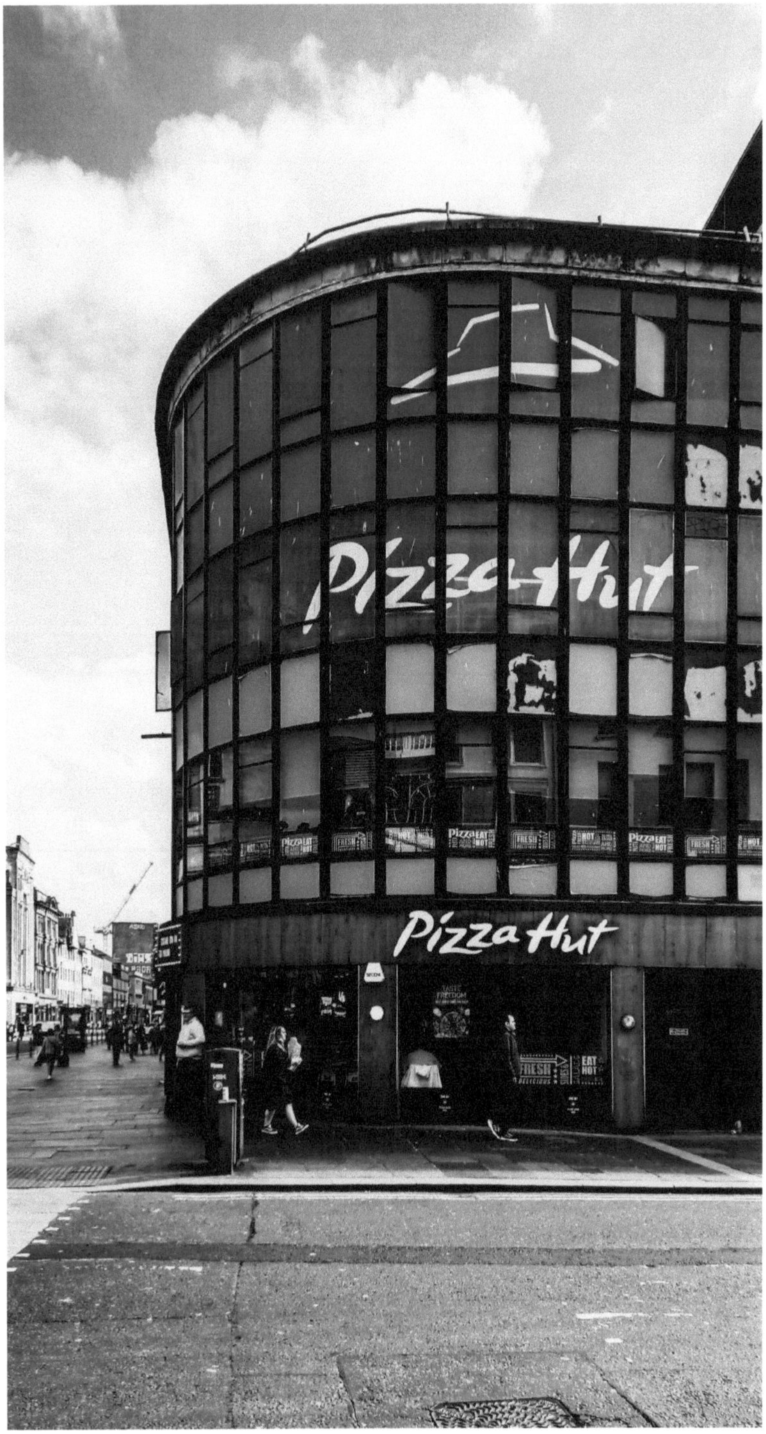
Pizza Hut
Pizza Hut

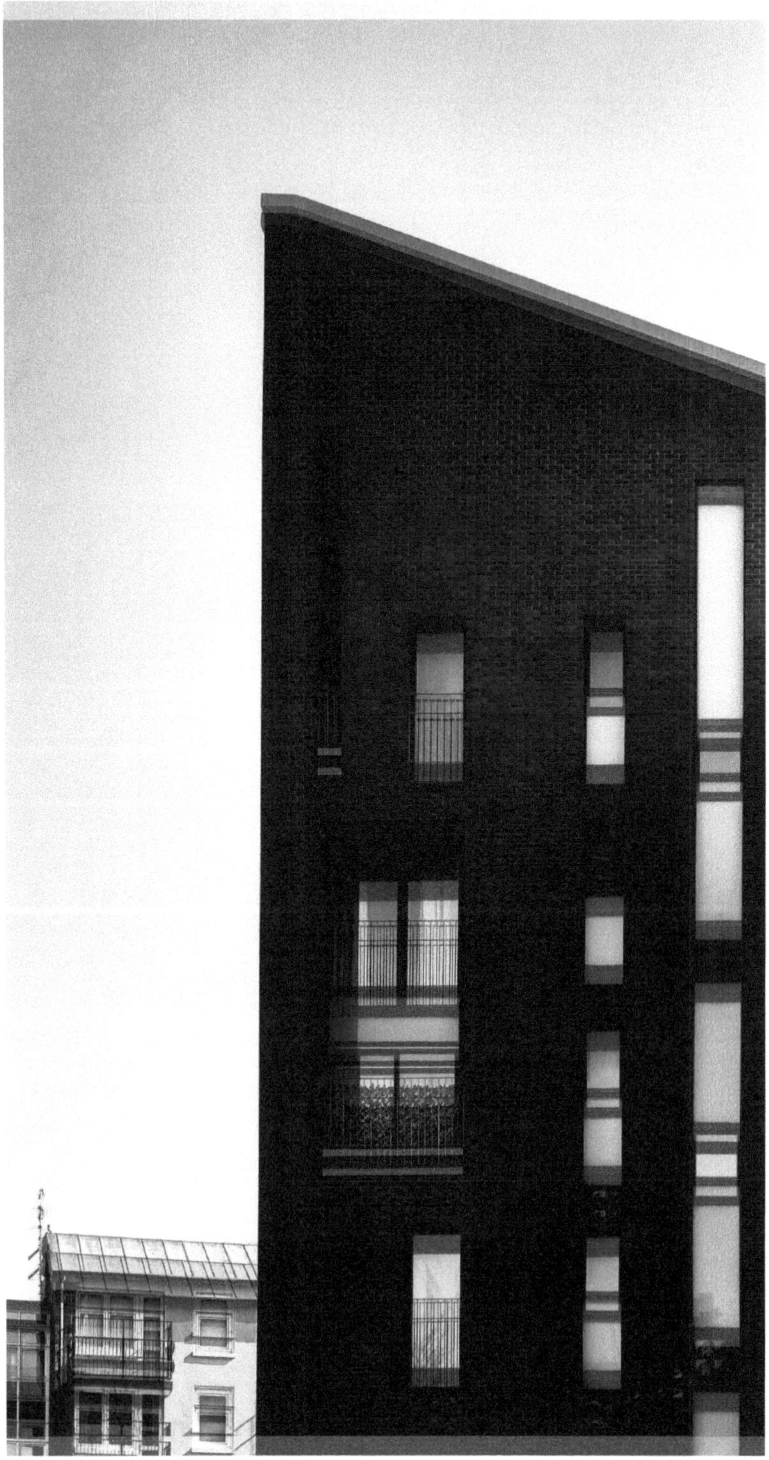

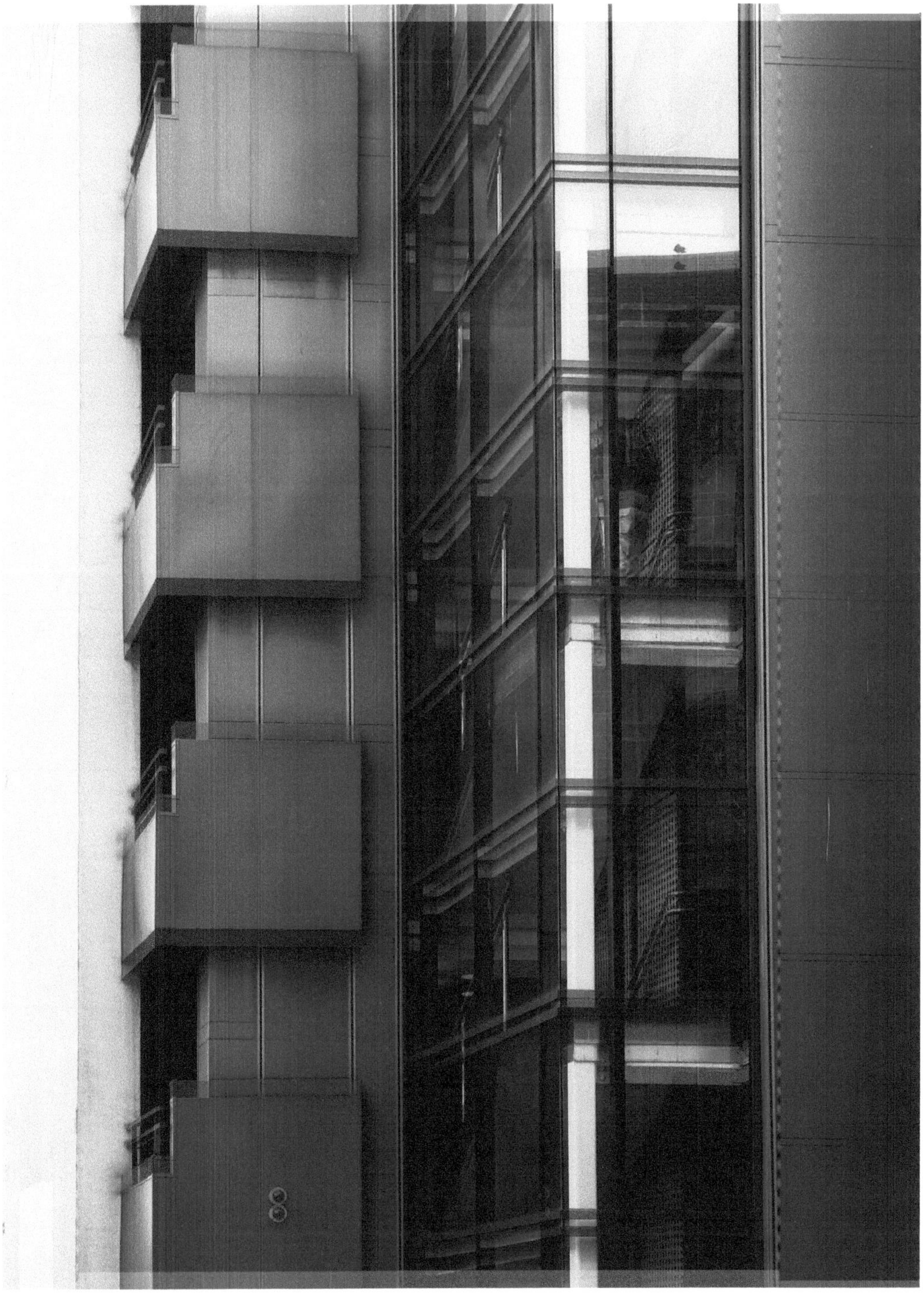

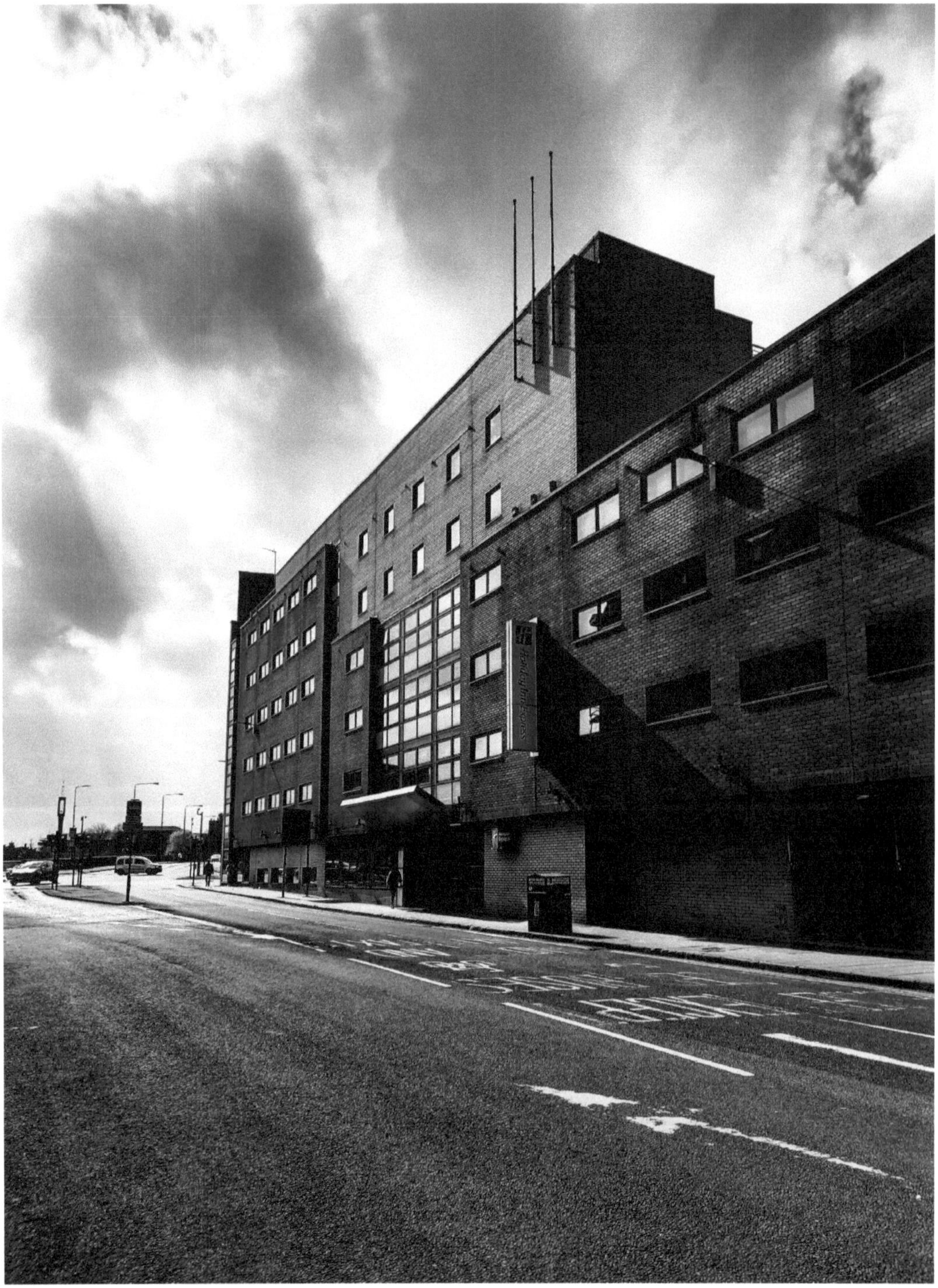

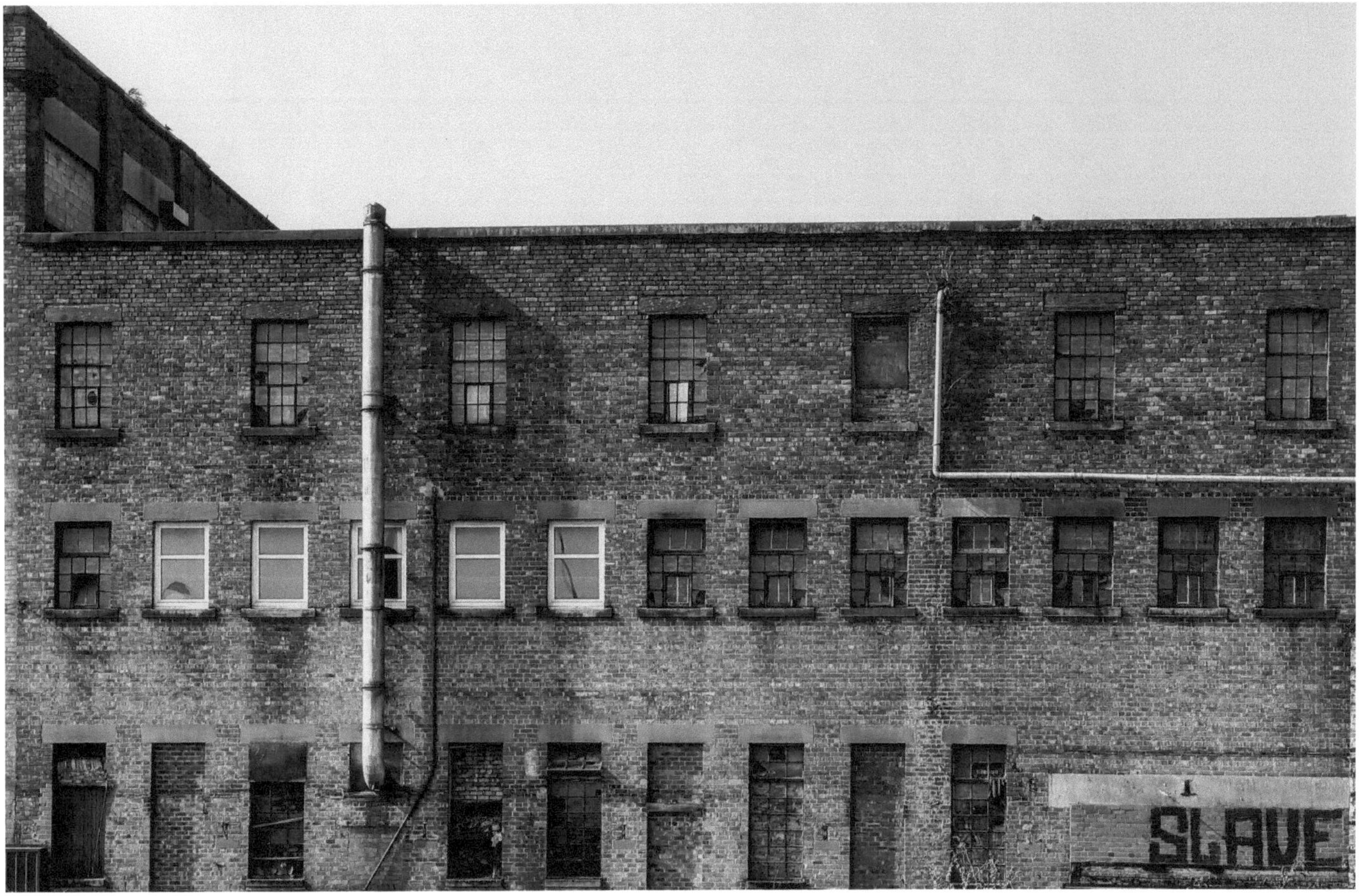
SLAVE

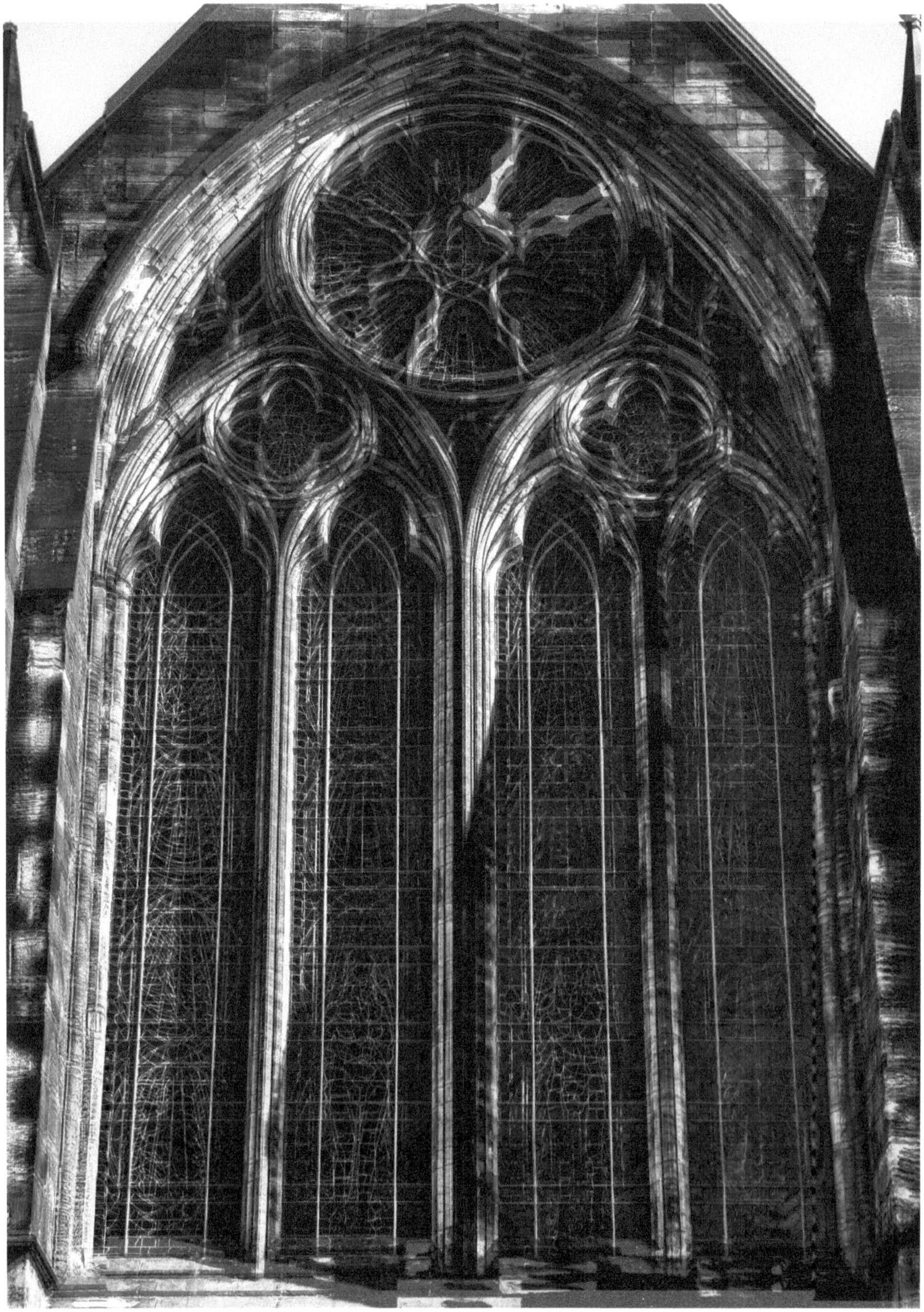

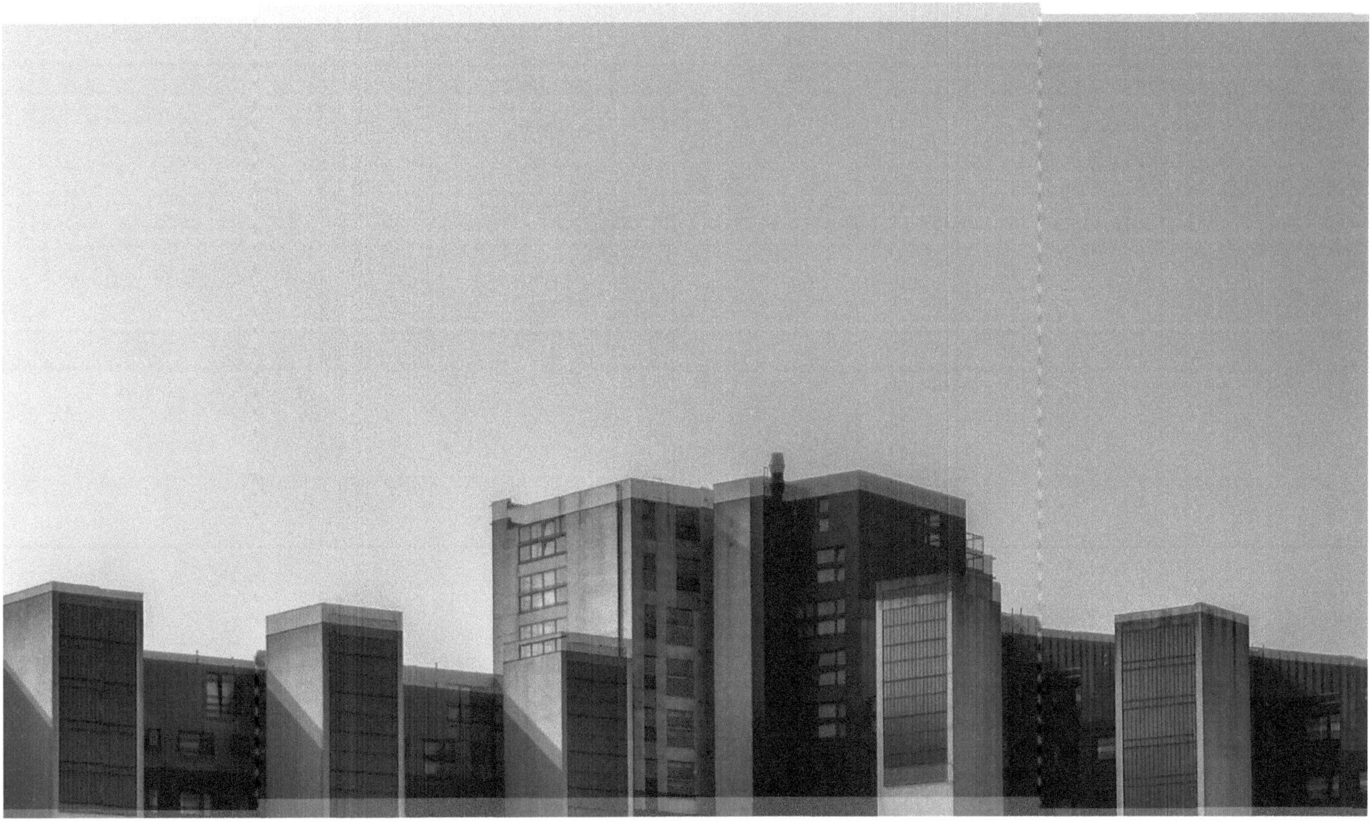

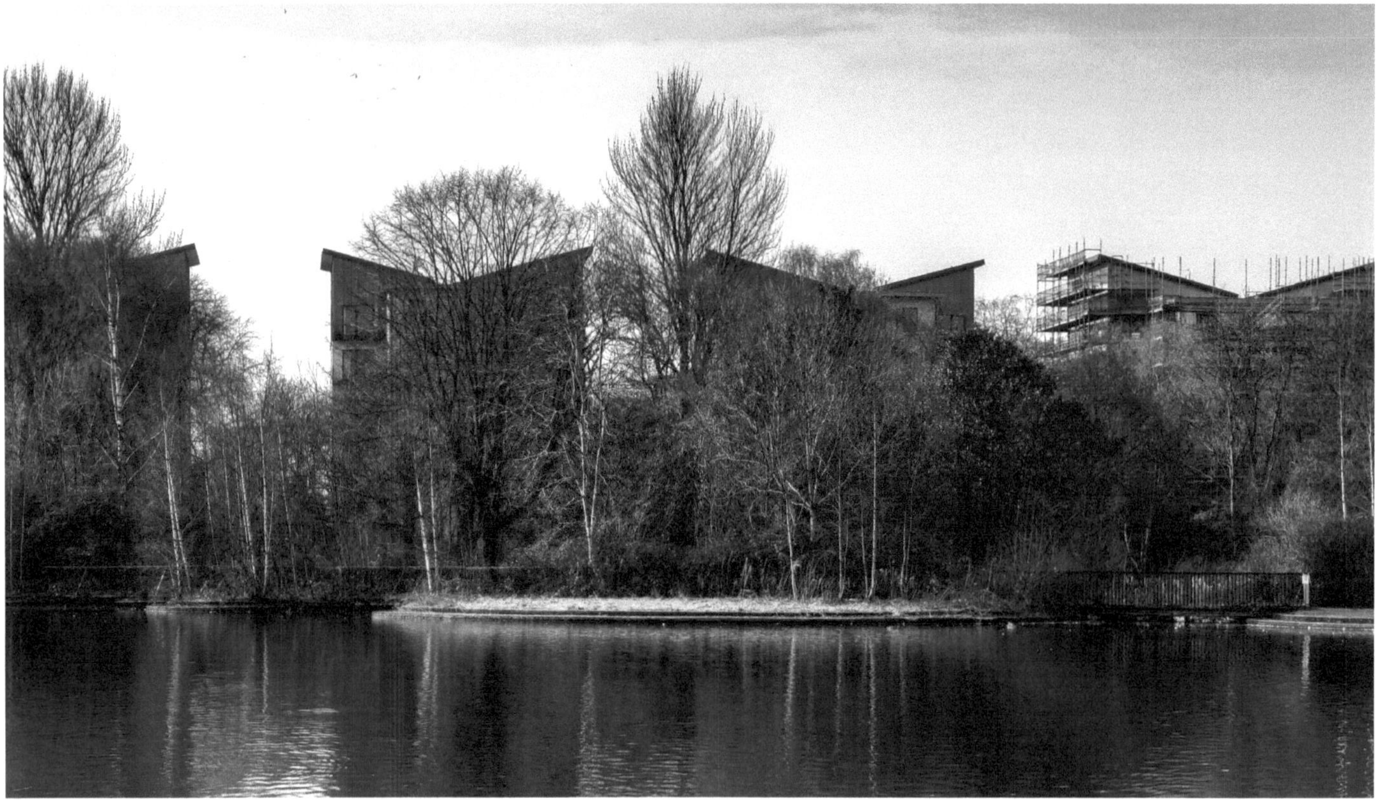

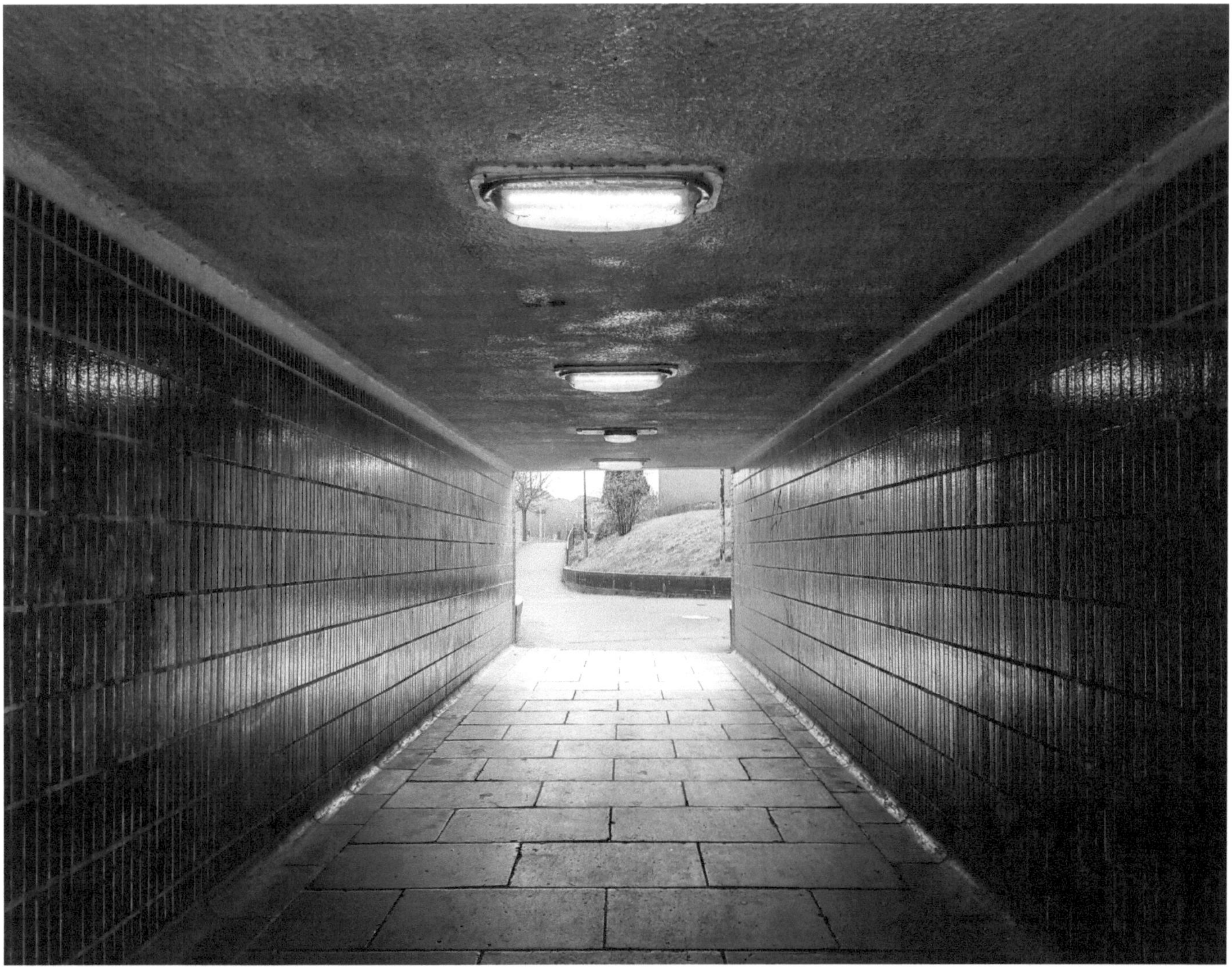

www.ingramcontent.com/pod-product-compliance
Lightning Source LLC
Chambersburg PA
CBHW051935210526
45473CB00006B/2258